SHAKESPEARIAN REFERENCES

P.V. GOPALAKRISHNAN

ATLANTIC PUBLISHERS AND DISTRIBUTORS

Published by
ATLANTIC PUBLISHERS AND DISTRIBUTORS
B-2, Vishal Enclave, New Delhi-110 027
Phones 5413460, 5429987

Sales Office
4346/4C, Ansari Road, Darya Ganj,
New Delhi-110 002
Phones 3273880, 3285873, 3280451
Fax 91-11-3285873
e-mail gupta.atlantc@axcess.net.in

ISBN 81-7156-772-X

Typeset at
APD Computer Graphics, Delhi
Printed in India at
Mehra Offset Press, Delhi

Shakespeare is a savage with sparks of genius which shine in a dreadful darkness of night.

— *Voltaire*

PREFACE

I was in a hospital when it first occurred to me the idea of preparing a reference book on Shakespearian quotations for the benefit of the common class. You may wonder at the expression 'hospital and manuscript'. No common bridge of human concept can be built between hospital and manuscript. But my particular health problem and my particular reference book were inter-woven itself in the form of symbiosis because mental agony was the root cause of my disease and it is an accepted fact, atleast in my experience, that Shakespearian references always are mind easing references. I am sure that persons who have a little knowledge of Shakespearian works will not hesitate to agree with me.

I had to spend one complete year for arraying some familiar quotations of Shakespeare under different heads. Three methods are used in this work to arrange the quotations. The widely used method of putting a reference under a particular title considering both the meaning and words was the main mode of selection. Some quotations are arranged by considering only a key-word to make sure the multiple use of this book. However this resulted in a defect that same quotations came under different heads as it bore more than one key-word. Some other references are accepted and arranged considering its meaning only. No key-words complying with the head can be seen in it.

Slight variations may be found in a few (only a few) references as slight variations are present among some texts which were used for the preparation of this book. It was my special interest to avoid unnecessary heads in order to reduce the pages so that this book will accessible to the common class.

Comments and suggestions from readers are welcomed for improving the standard of this book in the future editions.

P.V. GOPALAKRISHNAN

CONTENTS

ACT

Distill'd
Almost to Jelly with the act of fear.

— Hamlet

Ay me! what act,
That roars so loud, and thunders in the index?

— Hamlet

Some come to take their ease
And sleep an act or two.

— Henry VIII

Two truths are told,
As happy prologues to the swelling act of the imperial theme.

— Macbeth

Thyself shalt see the act;
For, as thou urgest justice, be assur'd
Thou shalt have justice, more than thou desir'st.

—The Merchant of Venice

Few love to hear the sins they love to act.

— Pericles

I do think there is mettle in death
which commits some loving act upon her,
she hath such a celerity in dying.

— Antony and Cleopatra

ADVERSITY

Let me embrace thee, sour adversity,
For wise man say it is the wisest course.

— King Henry VI

Sweet are the uses of adversity;
which like the toad, ugly and venomous,
wears yet a precious jewel in his head.

— As You Like It

Swen sorrows come, they come not single spies,
But in battalions.

— Hamlet

One woe doth tread upon another's heel,
So fast they follow.

— Hamlet

The worst is not
So long as we can say, "This is the worst".

— King Lear

There's small choice in rotten apples.

— The Taming of the Shrew

Misery acquaints a man with strange bedfellows.

— The Tempest

We have seen better days.

— Timon of Athens

Tomorrow, and tomorrow and tomorrow,
creeps in his petty pace from day to day
To the last syllable of recorded time.

— Macbeth

AFFECTION

Affection is a coal that must be cooled;
Else, suffered, it will set the heart on fire.

— *Venus and Adonis*

Affection! thy intention stabs the centre;
Thou dost make possible things not so held,
communicat'st with dreams.

— *The Winter's Tale*

'T is the curse of the service,
Permanent goes by letter and affection,
Not by the old gradation, where each second
stood heir to the first.

— *Othello*

And keep you in the rear of your affection.

— *Hamlet*

Then let thy love be younger than thyself,
or thy affection cannot hold the bent.

— *Twelfth Night*

Therefore the poet
Did feign that orpheus drew trees, stones, and floods;
Since nought so stockish, hard, and full of rage,
But music for the time doth change his nature.
The man that hath no music in himself,
Nor is not mov'd with concord of sweet sounds,
Is fit for treasons, stratagems, and spoils;
The motions of his spirit are dull as night;
And his affections dark as Erebus:
Let no such man be trusted.

— *The Merchant of Venice*

AGE

Crabbed age and youth cannot live together.

— The Passionate Pilgrim

I have lived long enough, my way of life
Is fall'n into the sear, the yellow leaf:

— Macbeth

Age cannot wither her, nor custom stale
Her infinite variety; other women cloy
The appetite they feed; but she makes hungry
where most she satisfies.

— Antony and Cleopatra

When the age is in, the wit is out.

— Much Ado About Nothing.

For you and I are past our dancing days.

— Romeo and Juliet

Past, and to come, seems best; things present, worst.

— Henry IV

The time is out of joint; O cursed spite,
That even I was born to set it right!

— Hamlet

So foul and fair a day I have not seen.

— Macbeth.

AIR

It is a nipping and an eager air.

— *Hamlet*

Love, whose month is ever may,
Spied a blossom passing fair,
Playing in the wanton air:

— *Love's Labour's Lost*

This castle hath a pleasant seat, the air
Nimbly and sweetly recommends itself
unto our gentle senses.

— *Macbeth*

Therefore the moon, the governess of floods,
Pale in her anger, washes all the air,
That rheumatic diseases do abound:

— *A Midsummer Night's Dream*

Trifles light as air
Are to te jeasous confirmations strong
As proofs of holy writ.

— *Othello*

The empty, vast, and wandering air.

— *Richard III*

Fair is foul, and foul is fair,
Hover through the fog and filthy air.

— *Macbeth*

ALL

My long sickness
of health and living now begins to mend,
And nothing brings me all things.

— *Timon of Athens*

Jack shall have Jill;
Nought shall go ill;
The man shall have his mare again,
and all shall be well.

— *A Midsummer Night's Dream*

All my pretty ones?
Did you say all? O hell-kite! All?
What! all my pretty chickens and their dam,
At one fell swoop?

— *Macbeth*

For Brutus is an honourable man;
So are they all, all honourable men.

— *Julius Caesar*

Death, as the psalmist saith, is certain
to all; all shall die. How a good yoke
of bullocks at stamford fair?

— *Henry IV*

All is not well;
I doubt some foul play.

— *Hamlet*

AMBITION

Cromwell, I charge thee, fling away ambition:
By that sin fell the angels;

— Henry VIII

Ambition should be made of sterner stuff.

— Julius Caesar

He that is proud eats up himself

— Troilus and Cressida

For he will never follow anything
That other men begin.

— Julius Caesar

Be not afraid of greatness. Some are born
great, some achieve greatness, and some
have greatness thrust upon them.

— Twelfth Night

If it were done when 'tis done, then't were well
It were done quickly.

— Macbeth

There is a tide in the affairs of men
which taken at the flood, leads on to fortune;
omitted, all the voyage of their life.
Is bound in shallows and in miseries.

— Julius Caesar.

A few, we happy few, we band of brothers.

— Henry V

ANGEL

And fights of angels sing thee to thy rest.

— Hamlet

I saw young Harry, with his beaver on,
His cushes on his thighs, gallantly armed,
Rise from the ground like feather'd mercury,
And vaulted with such ease into his seat,
As if an angel dropp'd down from the clouds,
To turn and wind a fiery pegasus,
And witch the world with noble horsemanship.

— King Henry IV

And let the angel whom thou still has served
Tell thee, Macduff was from his mother's womb.
Untimely ripp'd

— Macbeth

Two loves I have of comfort and despair
which like two spirits do suggest me still.
The better angel is a man right fair,
The worser spirit a woman colour'd ill.

— Sonnet-114

For Brutus, as you know, was Caesar's angel.

— Julius Caesar

Curse his better angel from his side
And fall to reprobation.

— Othello

Assume a virtue, if you have it not.
That monster, custom, who all sense doth eat,
Of habits devil, is angel yet in this.

— Hamlet

ANGER

Anger is like
A full-hot horse, who being allowed his way
Self-mettle tries him.

— King Henry VIII

Anger's my meat; I sup upon myself,
And so shall starve with feeding.

— Corio Lanus

Lay on, Macduff,
And damn'd be him that first cries "Hold, enough!"

— Macbeth

A countenance more in sorrow than in anger.

— Hamlet

O cassius! you are yoked with a lamb
That carries anger as the flint bears fire;
who much enforced, shows a hasty spark,
And straight is cold again.

— Julius Caesar

O! what a deal of scorn looks beautiful
In the contempt and anger of his lip.

— Twelfth Night

There is the moon, the governess of floods,
Pale in her anger, washes all the air,
That rheumatic diseases do abound:
And through this distemperature we see
The seasons alter, hoary-headed frosts
Fall in the fress lap of the crimson rose.

— A Midsummer Night's Dream

APPAREL

Costly the habit as thy purse can buy,
But not expressed in fancy, rich not gaudy,
For the apparel oft proclaims the man.

— *Hamlet*

Every true man's apparel fits your thief.

— *Measure for Measure*

What must the king do now? must he submit?
The king shall do it: must he be depos'd?
The king shall be contented: must he lose
The name of king? O' God's name, let it go.
I'll give my Jewels for a set of beads,
My gorgeous palace for a hermitage,
My gay apparel for an almsman's gown,
My figur'd goblets for a dish of wood,
My sceptre for a palmer's walking staff,
My subjects for a pair of carved saints,
And my large kingdom for a little grave,
A little little grave, an obscure grave;
Or I'll be buried in the king's highway,
Some way of common trade, where subjects' feet
May hourly trample on their sovereign's head;
For on my heart they tread now whilst I live;
And buried once, why not upon my head?

— *Richard II*

Take each man's censure, but reserve thy Judgment.
Costly thy habit as thy purse can buy,
But not express'd in fancy; rich, not gaudy;
For the apparel oft proclaims the man
And they in France of the best rank and station
Are most select and generous, chief in that.

— *Hamlet*

ARMS

If I must die,
I will encounter darkness as a bride,
And hug it in mine arms.

— Measure for Measure

Arms, take your last embrace! and, lips! O you
The doors of breath, seal with a righteous kiss
A dateless bargain to engrossing death.

— Romeo and Juliet

Time is like a fashionable host
That slightly shakes his parting guest by the hand,
And with his arms outstretch'd, as he would fly,
Grasps in the comer : welcome ever smiles,
And farewell goes out sighing.

— Troilus and Cressida

If he fight longer than he sees reason,
I'll forswear arms.

— Henry IV

Come the three corners of the world in arms,
And we shall shock them:

— Julius Caesar

ARTS

O! For a muse of fire, that would ascend
The brightest heaven of invention!

— Henry V

The play's the thing
Wherein I'll catch the conscience of the king.

— Hamlet

Exit, pursued by a bear.

— The Winter's Tale

If music be the food of love, play on

— Twelfth Night

I am never merry when I hear sweet music.

— The Merchant of Venice

Brevity is the soul of wit.

— Hamlet

An honest tale speeds best being plainly told.

— Richard III

The art of our necessities is strange,
That can make vile things precious.

— King Lear

I have as much of this in art as you,
But yet my nature could not bear it so.

— Julius Caesar

That he is mad, 'tis true; 'tis true; 'tis pity :
And pity 'tis', 'tis true; a foolish figure:
But farewell it, for I will use no art.

— Hamlet

When in disgrace with fortune and men's eyes
I all alone beweep my outcast state,
And trouble deaf heaven with my bootless cries,
And look upon myself and curse my fate,
Wishing me like to one more rich in hope,
Featur'd like him, like him with friends possessed,
Desiring this man's art, and that man's scope,
With what I most enjoy contented least;
Yet in these thoughts myself almost despising,
Happy I think on thee, and then my state,
Like to the lark at break of day arising
From sullen earth, sings hymns at heaven's gate:
For thy sweet love remember'd such wealth brings
That then I scorn to change my state with kings.

— *Sonnet-29*

Orpheus with his lute made trees,
And the mountain-tops that freeze,
Bow themselves when he did sing:
To his music plants and flowers
Ever sprung; as sun and showers
There had made a lasting spring
        Everything that heard him play,
        Even the billows of the sea,
        Hung their heads, and then lay by.
        In sweet music is such art,
        Killing care and grief of heart.
        Fall asleep, or hearing die.

— *King Henry VIII*

More matter with less art.

— *Hamlet*

There is no art
To find the mind's construction in the face;

— *Macbeth*

O! She's warm.
If this be magic, let it be an art
Lawful as eating.

— *The Winter's Tale*

Tir'd with all these, for restful death I cry,
As to behold seret a beggar born,
And needy nothing trimm'd in jollity,
And purest faith unhappily for sworn,
And gilded honour shamefully misplaced,
And maiden virtue rudely strumpeted,
And right perfection wrongfully disgrac'd,
And strength by limping sway disabled,
And art made tongue-tied by authority,
And folly-doctor-like-controlling skill,
And simple truth miscall'd simplicity,
And captive good attending captain ill;
Tir'd with all these, from these I would be gone,
Save that, to die, I leave my love alone,

— *Sonnet-66*

AUTHORITY

Wrest once the law to your authority:
To do a great right, do a little wrong.

— The Merchant of Venice

Study is like the heaven's glorious sun,
That will not be deep-search'd with saucy looks;
Small have continual plodders ever won,
Save base authority from others' books.

— Love's Labour's Lost

Merciful Heaven!
Thou rather with thy sharp and sulphurous bolt,
Split'st the unwedgeable and gnarled oak
Than the soft myrtle; but man, proud man,
Drest in a little brief authority,
Most ignorant of what he's most assur'd,
His glassy essence, like an angry ape,
Plays such fantastic tricks before high heaven,
As make the angels weep.

— Measure for Measure

KENT : You have that in your countenance which
I would fain call master.

LEAR : What's that?

KENT : Authority.

— King Lear

BEAR

This night, wherein the cub-drawn bear would couch,
The lion and the belly-pinched wolf keep their fur dry.

— King Lear

Approach thou like the rugged Russian bear,
The arm'd rhinoceros or the Hyrcan Tiger,
Take any shap but that, and my firm nerves
Shall never tremble.

— Macbeth

O, She will sing the savageness out of a bear.

— Othello

Exit, pursued by a bear.

— The Winter's Tale

We must bear all. O hard condition!

— Henry V

It hath been prophesied to me many years
I should not die but in Jerusalem,
Which vainly I suppos'd the Holy Land.
But bear me to that chamber; there I'll lie;
In that Jerusalem shall Harry die.

— Henry IV

BEAST

He grew into his seat,
And to such wondrous doing brought his horse,
As he had been incorps'd and deminatur'd
With the brave beast.

— *Hamlet*

The rugged pyrrhus, like the Hyrcanian beast.

— *Hamlet*

The beast
with many heads butts me away.

— *Coriolanus*

Kingdoms are clay; our dungy earth alike
Feeds beast as man; the nobleness of life
Is to do thus; when such a mutual pair
And such a twain can do't.

— *Antony and Cleopatra*

A very gentle beast, and of a good conscience.

— *A Midsummer Night's Dream*

Your daughter and the moor are now
making the beast with two backs.

— *Othello*

BEAUTY

Beauty is bought by judgment of the eye,
Not utter'd by base sale of chapmen's tongues.

— Love's Labour's Lost

Beauty's ensign yet
Is crimson in thy lips and in thy cheeks,
And death's pale flag is not advanced there.

— Romeo and Juliet

Beauty itself doth of itself persuade
The eyes of men without an orator.

— The Rape of Lucrece

A woman mov'd is like a fountain troubled,
Muddy, ill-seeming, thick, bereft of beauty.

— The Taming of the Shrew

O! She doth teach the torches to burn bright.
It seems she hangs upon the cheek of night
Like a rich Jewel in an Ethiop's ear;
Beauty too rich for use, for earth too dear.

— Romeo and Juliet

He hath a daily beauty in his life
That makes me ugly.

— Othello

One sees more devils than vast hell can hold,
That is, the madman; the lover, all as frantic,
Sees Helen's beauty in a brow of Egypt.

— A Midsummer Night's Dream

Ornament is but the guiled shore
To a most dangerous Sea; the beauteous Scarf
Veiling an Indian beauty; in a word,
To entrap the wisest.

— *The Merchant of Venice*

Could I come near your beauty with my nails
I'd set my ten commandments in your face.

— *Henry VI*

For where is any author in the world.
Teaches such beauty as a woman's eye?
Learning is but an adjunct to ourself.

— *Love's Labour's Lost*

And beauty, making beautiful old rhyme.

— *Sonnet, 106*

O! how much more doth beauty beauteous seem
By that sweet ornament which truth doth give!

— *Sonnet, 54*

Time doth transfix the flourish set on youth
And delves the Parallels in beauty's brow.

— *Sonnet, 60*

BED

Weary with toil, I haste me to my bed.

— *Sonnet, 27*

Here's flowers for you;
Hot lavender, mints, savory, marjoram:
The marigold, that goes to bed wi' the sun,
And with him rises weeping.

— *The Winter's Tale*

Although the sheet were big enough for
the bed of ware in England.

— *Twelfth Night*

Poor wounded name! my bosom, as a bed
Shall lodge thee till thy wound be thoroughly heal'd.

— *Two Gentlemen of Verona*

Item, I give unto my wife my second
best bed, with the furniture.

— *Will*

Not to be a— bed after midnight is to be
up betimes.... To be up after midnight
and to go to bed then, is early; so that
to go to bed after midnight is to go
to bed betimes.

— *Twelfth Night.*

Who in the lusty stealth of nature take
More composition and fierce quality
Than doth, within a dull, stale, tired bed,
Go to the creating a whole tribe of fops.

— *King Lear*

What! is Brutus sick,
And will he steal out of his wholesome bed
To dare the vile contagion of the night?

— Julius Caesar

What doth gravity out of his bed at midnight?

— Henry IV

Mine, and most of our fortunes, to-night,
Shall be, — drunk to bed.

— Antony and Cleopatra

But I will be
A bridegroom in my death, and run into 't
As to a lover's bed.

— Antony and Cleopatra

The tyrant custom, most grave Senators,
Hath made the flinty and steel conch of war
My thrice-driven bed of down.

—Othello

BIRTH

At my nativity
The front of heaven was full of fiery shapes,
Of burning cressets; and at my birth
The frame and huge foundation of the earth
Shak'd like a coward.

— *Henry IV*

His greatness weigh'd, his will is not his own,
For he himself is subject to his birth:

— *Hamlet*

I have't; it is engender'd; hell and night
Must bring this monstrous birth to the world's light.

— *Othello*

A gravions burthen was thy birth to me;
Tetchy and wayward was thy infancy.

— *Richard III*

Beauty, wit,
High birth, vigour of bone, desert in service,
Love, friendship, charity, are subjects all
To envious and calumniating time.

— *Troilus and Cressida*

BLESSING

I had most need of blessing, and "Amen"
Stuck in my throat.

— Macbeth

A double blessing is a double grace;
Occasion smiles upon a second leave

— Hamlet

Come, let's away to prison:
We two alone will sing like birds in the cage :
When thou dost ask me blessing, I'll kneel down,
And ask of thee forgiveness: and we'll live,
And pray, and sing, and tell old tales, and laugh
At gilded butterflies, and bear poor rogues.

— King Lear

Blessed are the peacemakers on earth

— King Henry VI

He gave his honours to the world again,
His blessed part to heaven, and slept in peace

—King Henry VIII

The blessed sun himself a fair hot wench in flame-coloured taffeta — I see no reason why thou shouldst be so superfluous to demand the time of the day.

— King Henry IV

In measure rain thy joy; scant this excess,
I feel too much thy blessing: make it less,
For fear I surfeit.

— The Merchant of Venice

BLOOD

A man whose blood
Is very snow-broth; one who never feels
The wanton stings and motions of the sense.

— *Measure for Measure*

Why should a man, whose blood is warm within,
Sit like his grandsire cut in alabaster?

— *The Merchant of Venice*

It will have blood, they say; blood will have blood:

— *Macbeth*

I am in blood
Stepp'd in so far that, should I wade no more,
Returning were as tedious as go o'er.

— *Macbeth*

Will all great Neptune's ocean wash this blood
Clean from my hand?

— *Macbeth*

Child Roland to the dark tower came,
His word was still, fie, Foh, and Fum,
I smell the blood of a British man.

—*King Lear*

You cannot call it love, for at your age
The hey-day in the blood is tame, it's humble
And waits upon the judgment.

— *Hamlet*

Am not I consanguineous? am I not
of her blood? Tillyvally, lady!

—*Twelfth Night*

I hate ingratitude more in a man
Than lying, vainnes, babbling drunkness,
or any taint of vice whose strong corruption
Inhabits our frail blood.

— *Twelfth Night*

O! blood, blood blood!

— *Othello*

On, on you noblest English!
Whose blood is fet from fathers of war-proof;

— *Henry V*

Thy bones are marrowless, thy blood is cold;
Thou hast no speculation in those eyes
which thou dost glare with.

— *Macbeth*

Your swords, made rich
With the most noble blood of all this world.

— *Julius Caesar*

BLOW

A word and a blow.

— Romeo and Juliet

Blow me about in winds! roast me in sulphur!
Wash me in steep-down gulfs of liquid fire!

— Othello

Blow, wind! come, wrack!
At least we'll die with harness on our back.

— Macbeth

Blow, winds, and crack your cheeks! rage! blow!
You cataracts and hurricanoes, spout
Till you have drench'd our steeples,
drown'd the cocks!

— King Lear

I must have liberty
Withal, as large a character as the wind,
To blow on whom I please.

— As You Like It

Blow, blow, thou winter wind,
Thou art not so unkind
As man's ingratitude.

— As You Like It

Lay me stark naked, and let the water-flies
Blow me into abhorring?

— Antony and Cleopatra

BODY

O! that this too too solid flesh would melt.
Thaw and resolve itself into a dew.

— *Hamlet*

I have more flesh than another man,
and therefore more frailty.

— *Henry IV*

To show . . . the very age and body of the
time his form and pressure.

— *Hamlet*

When the mind's free,
The body's delicate.

— *King Lear*

Fie, Fie upon her!
There's language in her eye, her cheek, her lip,
Nay, her foot speaks; her wanton spirits look out
At every joint and motive of her body.

— *Troilus and Cressida*

I would not have such a heart in my bosom
For the dignity of the whole body.

— *Macbeth*

And there at venice gave
His body to that pleasant country's earth,
And his pure soul unto his captain christ,
Under whose colours he had fought so long.

— *Richard II*

O England! model to thy inward greatness,
Like little body with a mighty heart,
What might'st thou do, that honour would thee do,
Where all thy children, kind and natural,
But see thy fault!

— *Henry V*

Make less thy body hence, and more thy grace;
Leave gormandising; know the grave doth gape
For thee thrice wider than for other men.

— *Henry IV*

By my troth, Nerissa, my little body is
aweary of this great word.

— *The Merchant of Venice*

Patch up thine old body for heaven.

— *Henry IV*

The soul and body rive not more in parting
Than greatness going off.

— *Antony* and *Cleopatra*

I never knew so young a body with so old a head.

— *The Merchant of Venice*

Thersites' body is as good as Ajax'
when neither are alive.

— *Cymbeline*

This common body,
Like to a vagabond flag upon the stream,
Goes to and back, lackeying the varying tide,
To rot itself with motion.

— *Antony* and *Cleopatra*

Fare thee well, great heart!
Ill-weav'd ambition, how much art thou shrunk!
When that this body did contain a spirit,
A kingdom for it was too small a bound:
But now two paces of the vilest earth
Is room enough: this earth, that bears thee dead,

Bears not alive so stout a gentleman.

— *Henry IV*

'Tis not the balm, the sceptre and the ball,
The sword, the mace, the crown imperial,
The intertissued robe of gold and pearl,
The forced title running 'fore the king,
The throne he sits on, nor the tide of pomp
That beats upon the high shore of the world,
No, not all these, thrice-gorgeous ceremony,
Not all these, laid in bed majestical,
Can sleep so soundly as the wretched slave,
Who with a body fill'd and vacant mind
Gets him to rest, cramm'd with distressful bread:

— *Henry V*

BOLDNESS

I dare do all that may become a man:
Who dares do more is none.

— *Macbeth*

I bear a charmed life.

— *Macbeth*

If it were done when 'tis done, then 't were well
It were done quickly.

— *Macbeth*

There is a tide in the affairs of men
Which, taken at the flood, leads on to fortune:
Omitted, all the voyage of their life
Is bound in shallows and in miseries.

— *Julius Caesar*

Be not afraid of greatness. Some are born
great, some achieve greatness, and some have
greatness thrust upon them.

— *Twelfth Night*

Cowards die many times before their deaths:
The valiant never taste of death but once.

— *Julius Caesar*

But screw your courage to the sticking place
And we'll not fail.

— *Macbeth*

And what makes robbers bold but too much lenity?

— *King Henry VI, Part II*

BOOKS

Was ever book containing such vile
matter so fairly bound?
Oh, that deceit should dwell in such a gorgeous palace!

— *Romeo and Juliet*

The bloody book of law
You shall yourself read in the bitter letter
After your own sense.

— *Othello*

He hath not fed of the dainties that
are bred in a book; he hath not eat
paper, as it were: he hath not drunk
ink.

— *Love's Labour's Lost*

The painful warrior famoused for fight,
After a thousand victories once foil'd,
Is from book of honour razed quite,
And all the rest forgot for which he toil'd.

— *Sonnet-25*

Deeper than did ever plummet sound,
I'll drown my book.

— *The Tempest*

I had rather than forty schillings I had
my Book of Songs and Sonnets here.

— *The Merry Wives of Windsor*

I nature's infinite Book of Secrecy
A little I can read.

— *Antony and Cleopatra*

O God! that one might read the book of fate.

— Henry IV

Thou hast most traitorously corrupted
the youth of the realm in erecting a
grammar school: and whereas, before, our
forefathers had no other books but the
score and the tally, thou hast caused
printing to be used; and, contrary to
the king, his crown and dignity, thou
has built a paper-mill.

— Henry VI

O! if this were seen
The happiest youth, viewing his progress through,
What perils past, what crosses to ensure,
Would shut the book, and sit him down and die.

— Henry IV

Your face, my thane, is as a book where men
May read strange matters. To beguile the time,
Look like the time: bear welcome in your eye,
Your hand, your tongue : Look like the innocent flower,
But be the serpent under't.

— Macbeth

From women's eyes his doctrine I derive:
They sparkle still the right promethean fire:
They are the books, the arts, the academes,
That show, contain, and nourish all the world.

— Love's Labour's Lost

From women's eyes this doctrine I derive:
They are the ground, the books, the academes,
From whence doth spring the true promethean fire.

— Love's Labour's Lost

Study is like the heaven's glorious sun,
That will not be deep-search'd with saucy looks;
Small have continual plodders ever won,
Save base authority from other's books.

These earthly godfathers of Heaven's lights
That give a name to every fixed star,
Have no more profit of their shining nights
Than those that walk and wot not what they are.

— *Love's Labour's Lost*

I see, lady, the gentleman is not in your books.

— *Much Ado About Nothing.*

The bookish theoretic

— *Othello*

One writ with me in sour misfortune's book.

— *Remeo and Juliet*

Knowing I lov'd my books, he furnish'd me,
From mine own library with volumes that
I prize above my dukedom.

— *The Tempest*

Love goes towards love, as school boys
From their books:
But love from love, towards school with heavy looks.

— *Romeo and Juliet*

Speaks three or four language word for
word without book.

— *Twelfth Night*

O! let my books be then the eloquence
And dumb presagers of my speaking breast.

— *Sonnet-23*

BORROWING

Neither a borrower nor a lender be:
For loan oft loses both itself and friend,
And borrowing dulls the edge of husbandry.

— Hamlet

He that dies pays all debts.

— The Tempest

I can get no remedy against this consumption
of the purse: borrowing only lingers and lingers
it out, but the disease is incurable.

— King Henry

I must become a borrower of the night
For a dark hour of twain.

— Macbeth

BOSOM

The sooty bosom
Of such a thing as thou.

— *Othello*

My bosom's lord sits lightly in his throne.

— *Romeo and Juliet*

One, two, and the third in your bosom.

— *Romeo and Juliet*

The sons of Edward sleep in Abraham's bosom.

— *Richard III*

Swell, bosom, with thy fraught,
For 'tis of aspics' tongues!

— *Othello*

The gaudy, blabbing, and remorseful day
Is crept into the bosom of the sea.

— *Henry VI*

Leave her to heaven,
And to those thorns that in her bosom lodge,
To prick and sting her.

— *Hamlet*

Cure her of that:
Canst thou not minister to a mind diseas'd,
Pluck from the memory a rooted sorrow,
Raze out the written troubles of the brain,
And with some sweet oblivious antidote
Cleanse the stuff'd bosom of that perilous stuff.
Which weighs upon the heart?

— *Macbeth*

The poor soul sat sighing by a Sycamore tree,
Sing all a green willow:
Her hand on her bosom, her head on her knee,
Sing willow, willow, willow:
The fresh streams ran by her, and murmur'd her moans:

— *Othello*

BOY

When that I was and a little tiny boy,
With hey, ho, the wind and the rain:
A foolish thing was but a toy,
For the rain it raineth every day.

— *Twelfth Night*

As flies to wanton boys, are we to the gods:
They kill us for their sport.

— *King Lear*

Hast thou no care of me? Shall I abide
In this dull world, which in thy absence is
No better than a stay? O! see me women,
The crown O' the earth doth melt. My lord:
O! withered is the garland of the war,
The soldier's pole is fall'n: young boys and girls
Are level now with men: the odds is gone,
And there is nothing left remarkable
Beneath the visiting moon.

— *Antony and Cleopatra*

And if the boy have not a woman's gift
To rain a shower of commanded tears,
An onion will do well for such a shift.

— *The Taming of the Shrew*

A parlous boy

— *King Richard III*

A corinthian, a lad of mettle, a good boy.

— *King Henry IV, Part I*

BREAST

On her left breast
A mole cinque-spotted, like the crimson drops.
I' the bottom of a cowslip.

— *Cymbeline*

What his breast forges, that his tongue must vent.

— *Coriolanus.*

Whereat, with blade, with bloody blameful blade,
He bravely braach'd his boiling bloody breast.

— *A Midsummer Night's Dream*

Sleep dwell upon thine eyes, peace in thy breast!
Would I were sleep and peace, so sweet to rest!

— *Romeo and Juliet*

The sea being smooth.
How may shallow bauble boats dare sail
Upon her patient breast.

— *Troilus and Cressida*

If snow be white, why then her breasts are dun;
If hairs be wires, black wires grow on her head.

— *Sonnet-130*

BROTHER

A bloody deed! almost as bad, good mother,
As kill a king, and marry with his brother.

— *Hamlet*

I have shot mine arrow o'er the house
And hurt my brother.

— *Hamlet*

I am sworn brother, Sweet,
To grim Necessity, and he and I
will keep a league till death.

— *Richard II*

O my poor brother!

— *Twelfth Night*

And what shall I do in Illyria?
My brother, he is in Elysium.

— *Twelfth Night*

Ha, ha! what a fool Honesty is! and
Trust his sworn brother, a very
Simple gentleman!

— *The Winter's Tale*

BUSINESS

We will proceed no further in this business:
He hath honour'd me of late; and I have bought
Golden opinions from all sorts of people.

— Macbeth

O! that a man might know
The end of this day's business, ere it come;
But it sufficeth that the day will end,
And then the end is known.

— Julius Caesar

Has this fellow no feeling of his business?

— Hamlet

My stronger guilt defeats my strong intent;
And, like a man to double business bound,
I stand in pause where I shall first began,
And both neglect.

— Hamlet

To business that we love we rise betime,
And go to't with delight.

— Antony and Cleopatra

CARE

Hast thou no care of me? Shall I abide
In this dull world, which in thy absence is
No better than a sty?

— *Antony and Cleopatra*

O polish'd perturbation! golden care!
That keep'st the ports of slumber open wide.
To many a watchful night!

— *Henry IV*

There is much care and valour in this welshman.

— *Henry V*

Macbeth does murder sleep, 'the innocent sleep,
Sleep that knits up the ravell'd sleave of care.

— *Macbeth*

What though care killed a cat, thou
hast mettle enough in thee to kill care.

— *Much Ado About Nothing*

Things past redress are now with me past care.

— *Richard II*

Crabbed age and youth cannot live together:
Youth is full of pleasance, age is full of care.

— *The Passionate Pilgrim*

CAUSE

The cause is in my will: I will not come.

— Julius Caesar

I am not only witty in myself, but the
cause that wit is in other man.

— Henry IV

Report me and my cause aright.

— Hamlet

It is the cause, it is the cause, my soul;
Let me not name it to you, you chaste stars!
It is the cause.

— Othello

But jealous souls will not be answer'd so;
They are not ever jealous for the cause,
But jealous for they are jealous.

— Othello

Their dearest action in the tented field;
And little of this great world can I speak;
More than pertains to feats of broil and battle;
And therefore little shall I grace my cause.
In speaking for myself.

— Othello

CHANGE

Since brevity is the soul of wit,
And tediousness the limit and outward flourishes.
I will be brief.

— *Hamlet*

Quietness, grown sick of rest, would purge
By any desperate change.

— *Antony and Cleopatra*

This world is not for aye, nor 'tis not strange,
That even our love should with our fortunes change.

— *Hamlet*

The lamentable change is from the best;
The worst returns to laugher.

— *King Lear*

All things that we ordained festival,
Turn from their office to black funeral;
Our instruments to melancholy bells,
Our wedding cheer to a sad burial feast,
Our solemn hymns to sullen dirges change,
Our bridal flowers serve for a buried corse,
And all things change them to the contrary.

— *Romeo and Juliet*

A man may see how this world goes with
no eyes. Look with thine ears; See how yond
Justice rails upon yond simple thief. Hark,
in thine ear: change places; and, handy-
dandy, which is the justice which is
the thief?

— *King Lear*

Nothing of him that doth fade
But doth suffer a sea-change
Into something rich and strange.

— *The Tempest*

The miserable change now at my end
Lament nor sorrow at; but please your thoughts
In feeding them with those my former fortunes
Wherein I liv'd, the greatest prince O' the world,
The noblest; and do now not basely die,
Nor cowardly put off my helmet to
My countryman; a Roman by a Roman
valiantly vanquished.

— *Antony and Cleopatra*

My desolation does begin to make
A better life. 'Tis paltry to be Caesar;
Not being Fortune, he's but Fortune's knave,
A minister of her will; and it is great
To do that thing that ends all other deeds,
Which shackles accidents, and bolts up change,
Which sleeps, and never palates more the dug,
The beggar's nurse and Caesar's.

— *Antony and Cleopatra*

CHANTICLEER

Some say that ever 'gainst that season comes
wherein our Saviour's birth is celebrated,
The bird of dawning singeth all night long.

— *Hamlet*

My lungs began to crow like chanticleer,
That fools should be so deep-contemplative,
And I did laugh sans intermission
An hour by his dial. O noble fool!
A worthy fool! Motley's the only wear.

— *As You Like It*

Come unto these yellow sands,
And then take hands:
Curtsier when you have, and kiss'd,
The wild waves whist,
Foot it featly here and there;
And, sweet sprites, the burden bear,
Hark, hark!
        Bow, wow,
The watch-dogs bark:
        Bow, wow,
Hark, hark! I hear
The strain of strutting chanticleer Cock-a-diddle-dow.

— *The Tempest*

CHASTITY

My chastity's the Jewel of our house,
Bequeathed down from many ancestors.

— *All's Well That Ends Well*

O ill-starr'd wench!
Pale as thy Smock! when we shall meet at compt,
This look of thine will hurl my soul from heaven,
And fiends will snatch at it. Cold, Cold, my girl!
Even like thy chastity.

— *Othello*

CHEEK

She never told her love,
But let concealment, like a worm i'the bud,
Feed on her damask cheek: she pin'd in thought:

— *Twelfth Night*

O! she doth teach the torches to burn bright.
It seems she hangs upon the cheek of night
Like a rich Jewel in an Ethiop's ear;
Beauty too rich for use, for earth too dear.

— *Romeo and Juliet*

Fie, Fie upon her!
There's language in her eye, her cheek, her lip,
Nay, her foot speaks; her wanton spirits look out
At every joint and motive of her body.

— *Troilus and Cressida*

See! how she leans her cheek upon her hand;
O! that I were a glove upon that hand;
That I might touch that cheek.

— *Romeo and Juliet*

The barber's man hath been seen with him;

and the old ornament of his cheek hath already stuffed tennis-balls.

— *Much Ado About Nothing*

Have you not a moist eye, a dry hand, a
Yellow cheek, a white beard, a decreasing
leg, an increasing belly?

— *Henry IV*

CHEER

Lay aside life-harming heaviness,
And entertain a cheerful disposition.

— *Richard II*

This push
will cheer me ever or disseat me now.
I have lived long enough: my way of life
Is fall'n into the sear, the yellow leaf;
And that which should accompany old age,
As honour, love, obedience, troops of friends,
I must not look to have; but, in their stead,
Curses, not loud but deep, mouth-honour-breath,
which the poor heart would fain deny, and dare not.

— *Macbeth*

CHILD

How sharper than a serpant's tooth it is
To have a thankless child!

— *King Lear*

In the father the child's image lies.

— *Rape of Lucrece*

A child of our grandmother eve, a female;
or, for thy more sweet understanding, a
woman.

— *Love's Labour's Lost*

Grief fills the room up of my absent child,
Lies in his bed, walks up and down with me,
Puts on his pretty looks, repeats his words,
Remembers me of all his gracious parts,
Stuffs out his vacant garments with his form.

— *King John*

As a decrepit father takes delight
To see his active child do deeds of youth,
So I, made lame by fortune's dearest spite,
Take all my comfort of thy worth and truth.

— *Sonnet-37*

Woe to the land that's govern'd by a child!

— *Richard III*

For, as I am a man, I think this lady
To be my child Cordelia.

— *King Lear*

O hateful error, melancholy's child!
Why dost thou show, to the apt thoughts of men,
The things that are not?

— *Julius Caesar*

It is a wise father that knows his own child.

— *Merchant of Venice*

He's in Arthur's bosom, if ever man
went to Arthur's bosom. A' made a
finer end, and went away and it had been
any christom child; a' parted even just
between twelve and one, even at the
turning o' the tide : For after I saw him
fumble with the sheets and play with
flowers and smile upon his fingers'
ends, I knew there was but one way:
for his nose was as sharp as a pen,
and a' babbled of green fields.

— *Henry V*

COME

Come, civil night,
Thou sober-suited matron, all in black.

— Romeo and Juliet

What's past, and what's to come, is
strew'd with husks.
And formless ruin of oblivion.

— Troilus and Cressida

Present mirth hath present laugher;
What's to come is still unsure;

— Twelfth Night

Come unto these yellow sands
And then take hands.

— The Tempest

Romeo, come forth; come forth, thou fearful man;
Affliction is enamour'd of thy parts,
And thou art wedded to calamity.

— Romeo and Juliet

The idea of march are come.

— Julius Caesar

No, no he is dead;
Go to thy death-bed,
He never will come again,

— Hamlet

CONFESS

Confess yourself to heaven:
Repent what's past; avoid what is to come;
And do not spread the compost on the weeds,
To make them ranker.

— *Hamlet*

Nor do we find him forward to be sounded,
But, with a crafty madness, keeps aloof,
When we would bring him on to some confession,
Of his true state.

— *Hamlet*

CONFUSION

Confusion now hath made his masterpiece!
Most sacrilegious murder hath broke ope
The Lord's anointed temple, and stole thence
The life O' the building!

— *Macbeth*

If there were sympathy in choice,
War, death, or sickness did lay siege to it,
Making it momentary as a sound,
Swift as a shadow, short as any dream,
Brief as the lightning in the collied night,
That, in a spleen, unfolds both heaven and earth.
And ere a man hath power to say "Behold"!
The Jaws of darkness do devour it up;
So quick bright things come to confusion.

— *A Midsummer Night's Dream*

CONSCIENCE

Thus conscience does make cowards of us all;
And thus the native hue of resolution
Is sicklied o'er with the pale cast of thought.

— *Hamlet*

Thou in the trade of war I have slain men,
Yet do I hold it very stuff o' the conscience,
To do no contriv'd murder: I lack iniquity
Sometimes to do me service.

— *Othello*

What stronger breastplate than a heart untainted!
Thrice is he arm'd that hath his quarrel just,
And he but naked, though lock'd up in steel,
Whose conscience with injustice is corrupted.

— *Henry VI*

A piece above all earthly dignities,
A still and quit conscience.

— *Henry VIII*

It seems the marriage with his brother's wife
Has crept too near his conscience.

— *Henry VIII*

The play's the thing
wherein I'll catch the conscience of the king.

— *Hamlet*

Conscience is but a word that cowards use,
Devis'd at first to keep the strong in awe.

— *Richard III*

Give me another horse! bind up my wounds!
Have mercy, Jesu! Soft! I did but dream.
O coward conscience, how dost thou afflict me!

— *Rechard III*

In venice they do let heaven see the pranks
They dare not show their husbands; their best conscience,
Is not to leave't undone, but keep't unknown.

— *Othello*

A very gentle beast, and of a good conscience.

— *A Midsummer Night's Dream*

Love is too young to know what conscience is;
Yet who knows not conscience is born of love?

— *Sonnet-151*

To hell, allegiance! vows, to the blackest devil!
Conscience and grace, to the profoundest pit!
I dare damnation.

— *Hamlet*

CONSTANCY

I am constant as the northern star,
Of whose true-fix'd and resting quality
There is no fellow in the firmament.

— Julius Caesar

O constancy! be strong upon my side;
Set a huge mountain 'tween my heart and tongue;
I have a man's mind, but a woman's might.
How hard it is for women to keep counsel!

— Julius Caesar

Constant you are,
But yet a woman; and for secrecy,
No lady closer; for I well believe
Thou wilt not utter what thou dost not know.

— Henry IV

Friendship is constant in all other things
Save in the office and affairs of love.

— Much Ado About Nothing

So, in the world; 'tis furnish'd well with men,
And men are flesh and blood, and apprehensive;
Yet in the number I do know but one
That unassailable holds on his rank,
Unshak'd of motion: and that I am he,
Let me a little show it, even in this,
That I was constant cimber should be banish'd,
And constant do remain to keep him so.

— Julius Caesar

COQUETTE

There's language in her eye, her cheek, her lip,
Nay, her foot speaks; her wanton spirits look out
At every joint and motive of her body.

— *Troilus and Cressida*

Thou hast never in thy life
Show'd thy dear mother any courtesy;
When she — poor hen! fond of no second brood-
Has cluck'd thee to the wars, and safely home,
Loaden with honour.

— *Coriolanus*

I am a very foolish, fond old man,
Fourscore and upward, not an hour more or less;
And, to deal plainly,
I fear I am not in my perfect mind.

— *King Lear*

At lovers' perjuries,
They say, Jove laughs. O gentle Romeo!
If thou dost love, pronounce it faithfully;
Or if thou think'st I am too quickly won,
I'll frown and be perverse and say thee nay,
So thou wilt woo; but else, not for the world.
In truth, fair Montague, I am too fond.

— *Romeo* and *Juliet*

COURAGE

Cowards die many times before their deaths;
The valiant never taste of death but once.

— *Julius Caesar*

But screw your courage to the sticking place
And we'll not fail.

— *Macbeth*

For courage mounteth with occasion.

— *King John*

Husband, I come;
Now to that name my courage prove my title!
I am fire and air; my other elements
I give to baser life.

— *Antony and Cleopatra*

Gloucester, 'tis true that we are in great danger;
The greater therefore should our courage be.

— *Henry V*

It illumineth the face, which, as a beacon,
gives warning to all the rest of this little
kingdom, man, to arm; and then the vital
commoners and inland petty spirits
muster me all to their captain, the heart,
who, great and puffed up with this retinue,
doth any deed of courage; and this valour
comes of sherris.

— *Henry IV*

COWARD

Cowards die many times before their deaths;
The valiant never taste of death but once.

— Julius Caesar

Art thou afeared
To be the same in thine own act and valour
As thou art in desire? Wouldst thou have that
which thou esteem'st the ornament of life,
And live a coward in thine own esteem?

— Macbeth

At my nativity
The front of heaven was full of fiery shapes,
Of burning cressets; and at my birth
The frame and huge of foundation of the earth,
Shak'd like a coward.

— Henry IV

I know not how,
But I do find it cowardly and vile,
For fear of what might fall, so to prevent
The time of life.

— Julius Caesar

A plague of all cowards, still say I.

— Henry IV

CRAFTINESS

I know a trick worth two of that.

— *Henry IV*

Friends, Romans, Countrymen, lend me your ears;
I come to bury Caesar, not to praise him.

— *Julius Caesar*

Suspicion all our lives shall be stuck full of eyes;
For treason is but trusted like the fox,
Who, ne'er so tame, so cherish'd, and lock'd up,
Will have a wild trick of his ancestors.

— *Henry IV*

Let thy tongue tang arguments of state;
Put thyself into the trick of singularity.
She thus advises thee that sighs for
thee. Remember who commended thy
yellow stockings, and wished to see
thee ever cross-gartered.

— *Twelfth Night*

It was always yet the trick of our
English nation, if they have a good
thing, to make it too common.

— *Henry IV*

CRIME

The robbed that smiles steals something from the thief.

— Othello

Yet who would have thought the old man
to have had so much blood in him?

— Macbeth

Murder most foul, as in the best it is,
But this most foul, strange, and unnatural.

— Hamlet

If you bethink yourself of any crime
Unreconcil'd as yet to heaven and grace,
Solicit for it straight.

— Othello

Let the great gods,
That keep this dreadful pother o'er our heads,
Find out their enemies now. Tremble, thou wretch,
That hast within thee undivulged crimes,
Unwhipp'd of justice.

— King Lear

He took my father grossly, full of bread,
with all his crimes broad blown, as Flush as May;
And how his audit stands who knows save heaven?

— Hamlet

The web of our life is of a mingled yarn,
good and ill together: our virtues would be
proud if our faults whipped them not; and
our crimes would despair if they were
not cherished by our own virtues.

— All's Well That Ends Well

CROWN

Uneasy lies the head that wears a crown.

— Henry IV

If chance will have me king, why, chance may crown me.

— Macbeth

With mine own tears I wash away my balm,
with mine own hands I give away my crown.

— Richard II

King Stephen was a worthy peer,
His breeches cost him but a crown;
He held them six pence all too dear,
with that he call'd the tailor lown.

— Othello

Then, happy low, lie down!
Uneasy lies the head that wears a crown.

— Henry IV

No ceremony that to great ones 'longs,
Not the king's crown, nor the deputed sword,
The marshal's truncheon, nor the judges robe,
Become them with one half so good a grace
As mercy does.

— Measure for Measure

His present and your pains we thank you for;
when we have match'd our rackets to these balls,
we will in France, by God's grace, play a set
shall strike his father's crown into the hazard.

— Henry V

CRUELTY

I must be cruel, only to be kind.

— Hamlet

Come you spirits...
And fill me from the crown to the toe, top full,
Of direst cruelty! make thick my blood;
... come to my woman's breasts,
And take my milk for gall, you murdering ministers!

— Macbeth

'Tis a cruelty
To load a falling man.

— Henry VIII

Get thee to yond same sovereign cruelty:
Tell her, my love, more noble than the world,
prizes not quantity of dirty lands.

— Twelfth Night

Farewell, fair cruelty.

— Twelfth Night

The expense of spirit in a waste of shame,
Is lust in action; and till action, lust
Is perjur'd, murderous, bloody, full of blame,
Savage, extreme, rude, cruel, not to trust.

— Sonnet-129

CRY

Hang out our banners on the outward walls:
The cry is still', They come'; our castle's strength
Will laugh a seige to scorn.

— *Macbeth*

Close pent-up guilts,
Rive your concealing continents, and cry
These dreadful summoners grace.

— *King Lear*

When we are born we cry that we are come
To this great stage of fools.

— *King Lear*

You common cry of curs! whose breath I hate
As reek o'the rotten fens,

— *Coriolanus*

Thou wilt fall backward when thou hast more wit;
Wilt thou not Jule? and, by my halidom,
The pretty wretch left crying, and said 'Ay'.

— *Romeo and Juliet*

O! the cry did knock
Against my very heart.

— *The Tempest*

CURSE

Weary se'n-nights nine times nine
Shall be dwindle, peake and pine.

— Macbeth

All the infections that the sun sucks up
From bogs, fens, flats, on prosper fall, and make him.
By inch-meal a disease.

— The Tempest

'Tis the curse of the service,
perferment goes by letter and affection,
Not by the old gradation, where each second
Stood heir to the first.

— Othello

Curse his better angel from his side,
And fall to reprobation.

— Othello

You taught me language; and my profit on't
Is, I know how to curse: the red plague rid you,
For learning me your language!

— The Tempest

O curse of marriage!
That we can call these delicate creatures ours,
And not their appetites. I had rather be a toad,
And live upon the vapour of a dungeon,
Than keep a corner in the thing I love
For others' uses.

— Othello

CUSTOM

But to my mind, though I am native here
And to the manner born, it is a custom
More honour'd in the breach than the observance.

— Hamlet

Assume a virtue, if you have it not.
That monster, custom, who all sense doth eat,
Of habits devil, in angel yet in this.

— Hamlet

We must not make a scarecrow of the law,
Setting it up to fear the birds of prey,
And let it keep one shape, till custom make it
Their perch and not their terror.

— Measure for Measure

I have very poor and unhappy brains for
drinking: I could well wish courtesy
would invent some other custom of
entertainment.

— Othello

The heaven themselves, the planets, and this centre
observe degree, priority, and place,
Insisture, course, proportion, season, form,
office, and custom, in all line of order.

— Troilus and Cressida

For herein fortune shows herself more kind
Than is her custom: it is still her use
To let the wretched man outlive his wealth,
To view with hollow eye and wrinkled brow
An age of poverty.

— The Merchant of Venice

DANCING

Come unto these yellow sands,
And then take hands;
Courtsied when you have, and kiss'd
(The wild waves whist)
Foot it featly here and there;
And, sweet sprites, the burthen bear.

— *The Tempest*

For you and I are past our dancing days.

— *Romeo* and *Juliet*

If you find him sad,
Say I am dancing; if in mirth, report
That I am sudden sick.

— *Antony* and *Cleopatra*

To dance attendance on their lordships pleasures.

— *Henry VIII*

She is your treasure, she must have a husband;
I must dance bare-foot on her wedding day,
And, for your love to her, lead open in hell.

— *The Taming of the Shrew*

Bid me discourse, I will enchant thine ear,
or like a fairy trip upon the green,
or, like a nymph, with long dishevell'd hair,
Dance on the sands, and yet no footing seen;
Love is a spirit all compact of fire,
Not gross to sink, but light, and will aspire.

— *Venus and Adonis*

DARKNESS

How like a winter hath my absence been
From thee, the pleasure of the fleeting year!
What freezings have I felt, what dark days seen!
What old December's bareness every where!

— Sonnet-97

For I have sworn thee fair, and thought thee bright,
Who art as black as hell, as dark as night.

— Sonnet-147

The Jaws of darkness do devour it up:

— A Midsummer Night's Dream

The motions of his spirit are dull as night,
And his affections dark as Erebus:

— The Merchant of Venice

I must become a borrower of the night
For a dark hour or twain.

— Macbeth

And often times, to win us to our harm,
The instruments of darkness tell us truths:

— Macbeth

DAWN

Night's candles are burnt out, and Jocund day
Stands tip-toe on the misty mountain-tops.

— Romeo and Juliet

It faded on the crowing of the cock.
Some say that ever 'gainst that season comes
wherein our saviour's birth is celebrated,
The bird of dawning singeth all night long;
And then, they say, no spirit can walk abroad;
The nights are whose some; then no planets strike,
No fairy takes, nor witch hath power to charm,
So hallow'd and so gracious is the time.

— Hamlet

Never sees horrid night, the child of hell,
But, like a lackery, from the rise to set
Sweats in the eye of phoebus, and all night
Sleep in Elysium; next day after dawn,
Doth rise and help Hyperion to his horse,
And follows so the ever-running year,
with profitable labour to his grave:
And, but for ceremony, such a wretch,
winding up days with toil and nights with sleep,
Hath the forehand and vantage of a king.

— Henry V

DAY

Finish, good lady; the bright day is done,
And we are for the dark.

— *Antony* and *Cleopatra*

Unarm, Eros; the long day's task is done,
And we must sleep.

— *Antony* and *Cleopatra*

Would I had met my dearest foe in heaven
Ere I had ever seen that day, Horatio!

— *Hamlet*

O day and night, but this is wondrous strange!

— *Hamlet*

What time the shepher'd, blowing of his nails,
Can neither call it perfect day nor night.

— *Henry VI*

The gaudy, blabbing, and remorseful day,
Is crept into the bosom of the sea.

— *Henry VI*

Thou art a summer bird,
which ever in the haunch of winter sings
The lifting up of day.

— *Henry IV*

It is the bright day that brings forth the adder;
And that craves wary walking.

— *Julius Caesar*

O! that a man might know
The end of this day's business, ere it come;
But it sufficeth that the day will end,
And then the end is known.

— *Julius Caesar*

In the posteriors of this day; which
the rude multitude call the afternoon.

— *Love's Labour's Lost*

Come what come may,
Time and the hour run through the roughest day.

— *Macbeth*

The wolves have prey'd; and look, the gentle day,
Before the wheels of phoebus, round about.

— *Much Ado About Nothing*

The worst is death, and death will have his day.

— *Richard II*

Night's candle are burnt out, and Jocund day,
Stands tiptoe on the misty mountain tops.

— *Romeo* and *Juliet*

DEATH

The undiscovered country, from whose bourn,
No traveller returns.

— *Hamlet*

Fear no more the heat o'the sun
Nor the furious winter's rages;
thou thy worldly task hast done,
Home art gone and ta'en thy wages.

— *Cymbeline*

After life's fitful fever, he sleeps well;
Treason has done his worst; nor steel nor poison,
Malice domestic, foreign levy,
Nothing can touch him further.

— *Macbeth*

The wearist and most loathed worldly life,
That age, ache, penury, and imprisonment
Can lay on nature, is a paradise
To what we fear of death.

— *Measure for Measure*

Come away, come away, death,
And in and cypress let me be laid;
Fly away, fly away, breath:
I am slain by a fair cruel maid.
My shroud of white, stuck all with yew,
O, prepare it!
My part of death, no one so true
Did share it.

— *Twelfth Night*

All that live must die,
passing through nature to eternity.

— *Hamlet*

Alas! poor yorick. I knew him, Horatio.

— *Hamlet*

Men must endure
Their going hence even as their coming hither.

— *King Lear*

A man can die but once. We owe God a death.

— *Henry IV*

Nothing in his life
Became him like the leaving it.

— *Macbeth*

How oft when men are at the point of death
Have they been merry.

— *Romeo and Juliet*

It is silliness to live when to live is torment.

— *Othello*

To be, or not to be — that is the question:
whether 'tis nobler in the mind to suffer.
The slings and arrows of outrageous fortune,
Or to take arms against a sea of troubles,
And by opposing end them.

— *Hamlet*

This passion, and the death of a dear friend,
would go near to make a man look sad.

— *A Midsummer Night's Dream*

DEEDS

If it were done when 'tis done, then 't were well
It were done quickly.

— Macbeth

How far that little candle throws its beams!
So shines a good deed in a naughty world.

— Merchant of Venice

Nothing will come of nothing.

— King Lear

My nature is subdued
To what it works in, like the dyer's hand.

— Sonnet-III

These deeds must not be thought
After these ways; so, it will make us mad.

— Macbeth

My deeds upon my head! I crave the law.

— The Merchant of Venice

'Tis well said again:
And 'tis a kind of good deed to say well:
And yet words are no deeds.

— Henry VIII

My master is of churlish disposition
And little recks to find the way to heaven
By doing deeds of hospitality.

— As You Like It

Foul deeds will rise,
Though all the earth o'erwhelm them, to men's eyes.

— Hamlet

DEFIANCE

Lay on, Macduff,
And damn'd be him that first cries "Hold, enough!"

— *Macbeth*

To hell, allegiance! vows, to the blackest devil!
Conscience and grace, to the profoundest pit!
I dare damnation.

— *Hamlet*

I dare do all that may become a man:
Who dares do more is none.

— *Macbeth*

If I dare eat, or drink, or breathe, or live,
I dare meet surrey in a wilderness,
And spit upon him, whist I say he lies,
And lies, and lies.

— *Richard II*

O! what men dare do! what men may do!
What men daily do, not knowing what they do!

— *Much Ado About Nothing*

What man dare, I dare;
Approach thou like rugged Russian bear.
The arm'd rhinoceros or the Hyrcan tiger,
Take any shape but that, and my firm nerves,
Shall never tremble.

— *Macbeth*

DELIGHT

The isle is full of noises,
Sounds and sweet airs, that give delight, and hurt not.

— *The Tempest*

We do not come as minding to content you,
Our true intent is. All for your delight, we are not here.

— *A Midsummer Night's Dream*

There sleeps Titania some time of the night,
Lull'd in these flowers with dances and delight;

— *A Midsummer Night's Dream*

The labour we delight in physics pain.

— *Macbeth*

With one auspicious and one dropping eye,
With mirth in funeral and with dirge in marriage,
In equal scale weighing delight and dole.

— *Hamlet*

To business that we love we rise betime,
And go to't with delight.

— *Antony and Cleopatra*

DESIRE

Hereafter, in a better world than this
I shall desire more love and knowledge of you.

— As You Like It

If thou and nature can so gently part,
The stroke of death is as a lover's pinch,
Which hurts, and is desir'd.

— Antony and Cleopatra

Nought's had, all's spent,
Where our desire is got without content;

— Macbeth

I will not choose what many men desire,
Because I will not jump with common spirits
And rank me with the barbarous multitude.

— The Merchant of Venice

Methinks I have a great desire to
a bottle of hay: good hays sweet
hay, hath no fellow.

— A Midsummer Night's Dream

Being your slave, what should I do but tend
Upon the hours and times of your desire?

— Sonnet-57

DESPAIR

O,what a rogue and pleasant slave am I.

— Hamlet

Tomorrow, and tomorrow, and tomorrow,
Creeps in this petty pace from day to day,
To the last syllable of recorded time.

— Macbeth

Two loves I have of comfort and despair,
Which like two spirits do suggest me still:
The better angel is a man right fair,
The worser spirit a woman colour'd ill.

— Sonnet - 144

I shall despair. There is no creature loves me;
And if I die, no soul will pity me;
Nay, wherefore should they, since that I myself
Find in myself no pity to myself?

— Richard III

Rash-embrac'd despair,
And shuddering fear, and green-ey'd Jealousy.

— The Merchant of Venice

Cut off even in the blossoms of my sin,
unhousel'd, disappointed, unanel'd,
No reckoning made, but sent to my account
with all my imperfections on my head,
O, horrible! o, horrible! most horrible!
If thou has nature in thee, bear it not.

— Hamlet

DEVIL

The devil can cite scripture for his purpose.

— *Merchant of Venice*

The prince of darkness is a gentleman.

— *King Lear*

What, man! defy the devil: consider, he's
an enemy to mankind.

— *Twelfth Night*

For here's a young and sweating devil here,
That commonly rebels.

— *Othello*

And thus I clothe my naked Villany
With odd old ends stol'n forth of holy writ,
And seem a saint when most I play the devil.

— *Richard III*

I look down towards his feet; but that's a fable.
If that thou be'st a devil, I cannot kill thee.

— *Othello*

Give me the daggers. The sleeping and the dead,
Are but as pictures; 'tis the eye of childhood
That fears a painted devil.

— *Macbeth*

What! can the devil speak true?

— *Macbeth*

Thus may we gather honey from the weed,
And make a moral of the devil himself.

— *Henry V*

Let the devil

Be sometime honour'd for his burning throne.

— Measure for Measure

O! while you live, tell truth, and shame the devil!

— Henry IV

Assume a virtue, if you have it not,
That monster, custom, who all sense doth eat,
Of habits devil, is angel yet in this.

— Hamlet

A' said once, the devil would have him about women.

— Henry V

Now I perceive the devil understands welsh.

— Henry IV

How agrees the devil and thee about thy
Soul, that thou soldest him on Good Friday
last for a cup of Madeira and a cold
capon's leg?

— Henry IV

'Tis too much prov'd— that with devotio's visage
And pious action, we do sugar o'er
The devil himself.

— Hamlet

To hell, allegiance! vows, to the
blackest devil!
Conscience and grace, to the profoundest pit!
I dare damnation.

— Hamlet

'Zounds! Sir, you are one of those that
will not serve God if the devil bid you.

— Othello

For I am one of those gentle ones that
will use the devil himself with courtesy.

— Twelfth Night

The devil damn thee black, thou cream-faced loon!
Where gott'st thou that goose look?

— Macbeth

I know that a woman is a dish for the gods, if the devil dress her not.

— Antony and Cleopatra

O thou invisible spirit of wine! if thou hast no name to be known by, let us call thee devil.

— Othello

Every inordinate cup is unblessed, and the ingredient is a devil.

— Othello

DISCRETION

The better part of valour is discretion.

— *Henry IV*

Let your discretion be your tutor.

— *Hamlet*

Let's teach ourselves that honourable stop,
Not to outsport discretion.

— *Othello*

Be not too tame neither, but let your own discretion be your tutor: suit the action to the word, the word to the action; with this special observance, that you o'erstep not the modesty of nature.

— *Hamlet*

Beauty is bought by Judgment of the eye,
Not utter'd by base sale of chapmen's tongues.

— *Love's Labour's Lost*

A Daniel come to judgment! yea, a Daniel!
O wise young judge, how I do honour thee!

— *The Merchant of Venice*

Young in limbs, in judgment old.

— *The Merchant of Venice*

Why, all the souls that were forfeit once;
And He that might the vantage best have took,
Found out the remedy. How would you be,
If He, which is the top of judgment, should
But judge you as you are?

— *Measure for Measure*

DOUBT

I am cabin'd, cribb'd, confined, boud in
To saucy doubts and fears.

— Macbeth

Doubt thou the stars are fire
Doubt that the sun doth move;
Doubt truth to be a liar;
But never doubt I love.

— Othello

Modest doubt is called
The beacon of the wise.

— Troilus and Cressida

Think'st thou I'd make a life of jealousy,
To follow still the changes of the moon
with fresh suspicions? No; to be once in doubt.
Is once to be resolved.

— Othello

I pull in resolution, and begin
To doubt the equivocation of the fiend
That lies like truth: 'Fear not, till Birnam wood
Do come to Dunsiname'.

— Macbeth

Yet this shall I ne'er know, but live in doubt,
Till my bad angel fire my good one out.

— Sonnet-144

DREAM

To sleep: perchance to dream; ay there's the rub;
For in that sleep of death what dreams may come,
When we have shuffled off this mortal coil,
Must give us pause.

— *Hamlet*

Mad in pursuit, and in possession so;
Had, having, and in quest to have, extreme;
A bliss in proof,-and prov'd, a very woe;
Before, a joy propos'd; behind, a dream
All this the world well knows; yet none knows well;
To shun the heaven that leads men to this hell.

— *Sonnet-129*

There is some ill — a brewing towards my rest,
For I did dream of money-bags to-night.

— *The Merchant of Venice*

But as the fierce vexation of a dream.

— *A Midsummer Night's Dream*

The very substance of the ambitions is
merely the shadow of a dream.

— *Hamlet*

Between the acting of a dreadful thing
And the first motion, all the interim is
Like a phantasma, or a hideous dream:
The genius and the mortal instruments
Are then in council; and the state of man,
Like to a little kingdom, suffers then
The nature of an insurrection.

— *Julius Caesar*

I have had a dream, past the wit of
man to say what dream it was.

— *A Midsummer Night's Dream*

Give me another horse! bind up my wounds!
Have mercy, Jesu! Soft! I did but dream.
O coward conscience, how dost thou afflict me!

— *Richard III*

We were as twinn'd lambs that did frist; the sun,
And bleat the one at the other; what we chang'd
Was innocence for innocence; we knew not
The doctrine of ill-doing, no, nor dream'd
That any did.

— *The Winter's Tale*

Not mine own fears, nor the prophetic soul
of the wide world dreaming on things to come,
Can yet the lease of my true love control,
Suppos'd as forfeit to a confin'd doom.
The mortal moon hath her eclipse endur'd,
And the sad angurs mock their own presage.

— *Sonnet-107*

Thou hast nor youth nor age;
But, as it were, an after-dinner's sleep,
Dreaming on both.

— *Measure for Measure*

The eye of man hath not heard, the ear
of man hath not seen, man's hand is
not able to taste, his tongue to conceive,
nor his heart to report, what my dream was.

— *A Midsummer Nigtht's Dream*

He is a dreamer; let us leave him: pass.

— *Julius Caesar*

I know thee not, old man: fall to thy prayers;
How ill white hairs become a fool and Jester!
I have long dream'd of such a kind of man,
So surfeit-swell'd, so old, and so profane.

— *Henry IV*

He spake of her as Dian had hot dreams,
And she alone were cold.

— *Cymbeline*

O God! I could be bounded in a nut-shell,
and count myself a king of infinite space,
were it not that I have bad dreams.

— *Hamlet*

For he is superstitious grown of late,
Quite from the main opinion he held once
of fantasy, of dreams, and ceremonies.

— *Julius Caesar*

O, I have pass'd a miserable night,
So full of ugly sights, of ghastly dreams,
That, as I am a Christian faithful man,
I would not spend another such a night,
Though 't were to buy a world of happy days,
So full of dismal terror was the time!

— *Richard III*

DRESS

Costly thy habit as thy purse can buy,
But not express'd in fancy; rich, not gaudy;
For the apparel oft proclaims the man.

— *Hamlet*

He was indeed the glass
wherein the noble youth did dress themselves.

— *Henry IV*

I know that a woman is a dish for the
gods, if the devil dress her not.

— *Antony and Cleopatra*

Old Adam's likeness, set to dress this garden.

— *Richard II*

From you have I been absent in the spring,
when proud-pied April, dress'd in all his trim,
Hath put a spirit of youth in every thing.

— *Sonnet-98*

Merciful Heaven!
Thou rather with thy shard and sulphurous bolt
Split's the unwedgeable and gnarled oak
Than the soft myrtle; but man, proud man,
Drest in a little brief authority,
Most ignorant of what he's most assur'd,
His glassy essence, like an angry ape,
Plays such fantastic tricks before high heaven,
As make the angels weep.

— *Measure for Measure*

DRINKING

And let me the canikan clink;
A soldier's but a man;
A life's but a span;
Why, then, let a soldier drink.

— *Othello*

O God, that men should put an enemy in their mouths to steal away their brains that we should, with Joy, pleasance, revel and applause, transform ourselves into beasts!

— *Othello*

I have very poor and unhappy brains for drinking; I could well wish courtesy would invent some other custom of entertainment.

— *Othello*

I will buy with you, sell with you, talk with you, walk with you, and so following: but I will not eat with you, drink with you, nor pray with you. What news on the Rialto?

— *The Merchant of Venice*

Drink down all unkindness.

— *The Merry Wives of Windsor*

We'll teach you to drink deep ere you depart.

— *Hamlet*

END

The end crowns all
And that old common arbitrator, time,
will one day end it.

— Troilus and Cressida

What can be avoided
Whose end is purpos'd by the mighty gods?

— Julius Caesar

I like not such grinning honour as sir
walter hath: give me life; which if I can
save, so; if not, honour comes unlooked for,
and there's an end.

— Henry IV

Let the end try the man.

— Henry IV

O! that a man might know
The end of this day's business, ere it come;
But it sufficeth that the day will end,
And then the end is known.

— Julius Caesar

Here is my journey's end, here is my butt,
And very sea-mark of my utmost sail.

— Othello

Go with me, like good angels, to my end;
And, as the long divorce of steel falls on me,
Make of your prayers one sweet sacrifice,
And lift my soul to heaven.

— Henry VIII

They say he made a good end.

— *Hamlet*

He makes a swan-like end
Fading in music.

— *The Merchant of Venice*

ENGLAND

Once more into the breach, dear friends, once more,
Or close the wall up with our English dead!

— *Henry V*

This England never did, nor never shall,
Lie at the proud foot of a conqueror.

— *King John*

The game's afoot
Follow your spirit, and upon this charge
Cry "God for Harry, England, and Saint George!"

— *Henry V*

This royal throne of kings, this sceptered isle,
This happy breed of men, this little world.
This precious stone set in the silver sea,
This blessed plot, this earth, this realm, this England.

— *Richard II*

England, where indeed they are most potent in potting.

— *Othello*

That England, that was wont to conquer others,
Hath made a shameful conquest of itself.

— *Richard II*

EVIL

The evil that men do lives after them;
The good is oft interred with their bones.

— Julius Caesar

If one good deed in all my life I did,
I do repent it from my very soul.

— Titus Andronicus

The lady doth protect too much, methinks.

— Hamlet

Here's the smell of the blood still. All the perfumes of Arabia will not sweeten this little hand.

— Macbeth

Tempt not a desperate man.

— Romeo and Juliet

It's a bawdy planet.

— The Winter's Tale

Commit
The oldest sins the newest kind of ways.

— Henry IV

Lay on, Macduff,
And damn'd be him that first cries "Hold, enough!"

— Macbeth

There's small choice in rotten apples.

— The Taming of the Shrew

The worst is not
So long as we can say, "This is the worst"

— King Lear

Can one desire too much of a good thing?

— As You Like It

These violent delights have violent ends.

— Romeo and *Juliet*

There is some soul of goodness in things evil,
Would men observingly distil it out.

— Henry V

Men's evil manners live in brass; their virtues.
We write in water.

— Henry VIII

O benefit of ill! now I find true
That better is by evil still made better.

— Sonnet-119

So may the outward shows be least themselves;
The world is still deceived with ornament.
I law, what plea so tainted and corrupt
But, being season'd with a gracious voice,
obscureres the show of evil? In religion,
what damned error, but some sober brow
will bless it and approve it with a text,
Hiding the grossness with fair ornament?

— The Merchant of Venice

There is an old poor man,
oppress'd with two weak evils, age and hunger.

— As You Like It

EXCESS

To gild refined gold, to paint the lily,
To throw a perfume on the violet,
To smooth the ice, or add another hue
Unto the rainbow, or with taper-light
To seek the bear teous eye of heaven to garnish,
Is wasteful and ridiculous excess.

— *King John*

Can one desire too much of a good thing?

— *As You Like It*

These violent delights have violent ends.

— *Romeo and Juliet*

If music be the food of love, play on;
Give me excess of it, that, surfeiting,
The appetite may sicken, and so die.
That strain again! it had a dying fall:
O! it came o'er my ear like the sweet sound
That breathes upon a bank of violets,
Stealing and giving odour! Enough! no more:
'Tis not so sweet now as it was before.
O spirit of love! how quick and fresh art thou,
That notwithstanding thy capacity
Receiveth as the sea, nought enters there,
Of what validity and pitch Soe'er,
But falls into abatement and low price,
Even in a minute: So full of shapes is fancy,
That it alone is high fantastical.

— *Twelfth Night*

EYE

Sin of self-love possesseth all mine eye.

— Sonnet-62

Full many a glorious morning have I seen
Flatter the mountain-tops with sovereign eye,
Kissing with golden face the meadows green,
Gilding pale streams with heavenly alchemy.

— Sonnet-33

Fie, fie upon her!
There's language in her eye, her cheek, her lip,
Nay, her foot speaks; her wanton spirits look out,
At every joint and motive of her body.

— Triolus and Cressida

All places that the eye of heaven visits
Are to a wise man ports and happy havens,
Teach thy necessity to reason thus;
There is no virtue like necessity.

— Richard II

I have a good eye, uncle: I can see a church by daylight.

— Much Ado About Nothing

The eye of man hath not heard, the
ear of man hath not seen, man's hand
is not able to taste, his tongue to
conceive, nor his heart to report, what
my dream was.

— A Midsummer Night's Dream

A hell! to choose love by another's eye.

— A Midsummer Night's Dream

It is still her use
To let the wretched man outlive his wealth,
To view with hollow eye and wrinkled brow.
An age of poverty.

— *The Merchant of Venice*

Eye of newt and toe of frog.
Wool of bat and tongue of dog.

— *Macbeth*

Beauty is bought by judgment of the eye,
Not utter'd by base sale of chapmen's tongues.

— *Love's Labour's Lost*

For where is any author in the world
Teaches such beauty as a woman's eye?

— *Love's Labour's Lost*

The heavenly rhetoric of thine eye.

— *Love's Labour's Lost*

Set honour in one eye and death 'n the other,
And I will look on both indifferently.

— *Julius Caesar*

Unthread the rude eye of rebellion,
And welcome home again discarded faith.

— *King John*

A still-soliciting eye.

— *King Lear*

Have you not a moist eye, a dry hand,
a yellow cheek, a white beard, a
decreasing leg, an increasing belly?

— *Henry IV*

In my mind's eye, Horatio.

— *Hamlet*

Good Hamlet, cast thy nighted colour off,
And let thine eye look like a friend on Denmark.

— *Hamlet*

FACE

There's no art
To find the mind's construction in the face.

— Macbeth

The element itself, till seven years' heat,
shall not behold her face at ample view;
But, like a cloistress, she will veiled walls,
And water once a day her chamber round
with eye-offending brine.

— Twelfth Night

Away, and mock the time with fairest show:
False face must hide what the false heart doth know.

— Macbeth

And then my husband-God be with his soul!
A' was a merry man — took up the child;
'Yea', quoth he, 'dost thou fall upon thy face?
Thou wilt fall backward when thou hast more wit;
Wilt thou not, Jule? 'and, by my halidom,
The pretty wretch left crying, and said 'Ay'.

— Romeo and Juliet

I have heard of your paintings too,
well enough. God hath given you one face, and
you make yourselves another.

— Hamlet

Give me my Romeo: and, when he shall die,
Take him and cut him out in little stars,
And he will make the face of heaven so fine
That all the world will be in love with night,
And pay no worship to the garish sun.

— Romeo and Juliet

Thou know'st the mask of night is on my face,
Else would a maiden blush bepaint my cheek.

— *Romeo and Juliet*

Your face, my thane, is as a book where men
May read strange matters. To beguile the time,
Look like the time; bear welcome in your eye,
Your hand, your tongue: look like the innocent flower,
But be the serpent under't.

— *Macbeth*

Call you that backing of your friends?
A plague upon such backing! give me them
that will face me.

— *Henry IV*

Now entertain conjecture of a time
when creeping murmur and the poring dark,
Fills the wide vessel of the universe.
From camp to camp, through the foul womb of night,
The hum of either army stilly sounds,
That the fix'd sentinels almost receive
The secret whispers of each other's watch.
Fire answers fire, and through their play flames
Each battle sees the other's umber'd face;
Steed threatens steed, in high and boastful neighs,
Piercing the night's dull ear; and from the tents
The armourers, accomplishing the knights,
With busy hammers closing rivets up,
Give dreadful note of preparation.

— *Henry V*

FAIRIES

Where the bee sucks, there suck I.
In the cowslip's bell I lie;
There I couch when owls do cry.
On the bat's back I do fly
After summer merrily.

— *The Tempest*

Fairies, black, grey, green, and white,
You moonshine revellers, and shades of night.

— *The Merry Wives of Windsor*

You spotted snakes with double tongue,
Thorny hedge-hogs, be not seen;
Newts, and blind-worms, do not wrong;
Come not near our fairy queen.

— *A Midsummer Night's Dream*

The iron tongue of midnight hath told twelve;
Lovers, to bed; 'tis almost fairy time.

— *A Midsummer Night's Dream*

Bid me discourse, I will enchant thine ear,
or like a fairy trip upon the green,
or, like a nymph, with long dishevell'd hair,
Dance on the sands, and yet no footing seen:
Love is a spirit all compact of fire,
Not gross to sink, but light, and will aspire.

— *Venus and Adonis*

The nights are wholesome; then no planets strike,
No fairy takes, nor witch hath power to charm,
So hallow'd and so gracious is the time.

— *Hamlet*

FAITH

If I break faith, this word shall speak for me,
I am forsworn 'on mere necessity;'

— Love's Labour's Lost

When love begins to sicken and decay,
It useth an enforced ceremony.
There are no tricks in plain and simple faith.

— Julius Caesar

Unthread the rude eye of rebellion,
And welcome home again discarded faith.

— King John

And such a deal of Skimble-Skamble stuff
As puts me from my faith.

— Henry IV

It is to be all made of faith and service.

— As You Like It

My life upon her faith!

— Othello

And needy nothing trimm'd in jollity,
And purest faith unhappily forsworn,

— Sonnet-66

FALL

O, what a fall was there, my countrymen!
Then I, and you, and all of us fell down.

— *Julius Caesar*

Some rise by sin, and some by virtue fall

— *Measure for Measure*

Here wast thou bay'd, brave hart;
Here didst thou fall; and here thy hunters stand,
Sign'd in thy spoil, and crimson'd in thy leth.
O world! thou wast the forest to this hart;
And this, indeed, O world! the heart of thee.

— *Julius Caesar*

O spirit of love! how quick and fresh art thou,
That notwithstanding thy capacity
Receiveth as the sea, nought enters there,
Of what validity and pitch soe'er,
But falls into abatement and low price,
Even in a minute: so full of shapes is fancy,
That it alone is high fantastical.

— *Twelfth Night*

Not a whit, we defy augury; there's a
special providence in the fall of a sparrow.
If it be now, 'tis not to come; if it be
not to come, it will be now; if it be
not now, yet it will come; the readiness is all.

— *Hamlet*

'Tis one thing to be tempted, Escalus,
Another thing to fall. I not deny,

The Jury, passing on the prisoner's life,
May in the sworn twelve have a thief or two
Guiltier than him they try.

— *Measure for Measure*

FAMILY

Crabbed age and youth cannot live together:
Youth is full of pleasance, age is full of care.

— *Passionate Pilgrim*

O! he's as tedious
As a tired horse, a railing wife;
worse than a smoky house. I had rather live
with cheese and garlic in a windmill, far,
Than feed on cates and have him talk to me
In any summer-house in christendom.

— *Henry IV*

Let the doors be shut upon him, that he
may play the fool nowhere but in's own house.

— *Hamlet*

You take my house when you do take the prop
That doth sustain my house; you take my life
when you do take the means whereby I live.

— *The Merchant of Venice*

O! it comes o'er my memory,
As doth the raven o'er the infected house,
Boding to all.

— *Othello*

There's nothing ill can dwell in such a temple:
If the ill spirit have so fair a house,
Good things will strive to dwell with 't.

— *The Tempest*

FANCY

Tell me where is fancy bred,
Or in the heart or in the head?.
How begot, how hourished?
Reply, Reply.
It is engender'd in the eyes,
with gazing fed; and fancy dies
In the cradle where it lies.

— *Merchant of Venice*

Chewing the food of sweet and bitter fancy.

— *As You Like It*

He hath borne me on his back a
thousand times; and now, how abhorred in
my imagination it is! My gorge
rises at it.

— *Hamlet*

Costly thy habit as thy purse can buy,
But not express'd in fancy; rich, not gaudy;
For the apparel oft proclaims the man,
And they in France of the best rank and station
Are most select and generous, chief in that.

— *Hamlet*

O Spirit of love! how quick and fresh art thou,
That notwithstanding thy capacity
Receiveth as the sea, nought enters there,
of what validity and pitch soe'er,
But falls into abatement and low price,
Even in a minute: so full of shapes is fancy,
That it alone is high fantastical.

— *Twelfth Night*

FAREWELL

Farewell the tranquil mind farewell content
Farewell the plumed troop and the big wars,
That make ambition virtue! O, Farewell!
Farewell the neighing steed, and the shrill trump,
The spirit-stirring drum, the ear-piercing fife,
The royal banner and all quality
pride, pomp and circumstance of glorious war
And, O you mortal engines, whose rude throats
The immortal Jove's dread clamours counterfeit,
Farewell! Othello's occupation's gone!

— *Othello*

Fain would I dwell on form, fain, fain deny
what I have spoke; but farewell compliment!

— *Romeo and Juliet*

Time is like a fashionable host
That slightly shakes his parting guest by the hand,
And with his arms outstretch'd, as he would fly,
Grasps in the comer; welcome ever smiles,
And Farewell goes out sighing.

— *Troilus and Cressida*

Farewell, fair cruelty.

— *Twelfth Night*

Contempt, Farewell! and maiden pride, adieu!
No glory lives behind the back of such.
And, Benedick, love on : I will requite thee,
Taming my wild heart to thy loving hand.

— *Much Ado About Nothing*

Farewell, and stand fast.

— *Henry IV*

That he is mad, 'tis true; 'tis true 'tis pity;
And pity 'tis 'tis true; a foolish figure;
But Farewell it, for I will use no art

— *Hamlet*

Sweets to the sweet : Farewell!

— *Hamlet*

Thy ignominy sleep with thee in the grave,
But not remember'd in thy epitaph!
What! old acquaintance! could not all this flesh
Keep in a little life? poor Jack, farewell!
I could have better spar'd a better man.

— *Henry IV*

And whether we shall meet again, I know not
Therefore our everlasting farewell take:

— *Julius Caesar*

FASHION

The glass of fashion, and the mould of form,
The observed of all observers.

— Hamlet

The fashion wears out more apparel than the man.

— Much Ado About Nothing

The apparel oft proclaims the man.

— Hamlet

Perseverance, dear my lord,
Keeps honour bright: to have done, is to hang
Quite out of fashion, like a rusty mail
In monumental mockery.

— Troilus and Cressida

Lie ten nights awake, carving the fashion
of a new doublet.

— Much Ado About Nothing

You, Sir, I entertain for one of my
hundred; only I do not like the fashion
of your garments: you will say, they are
Persian attire; but let them be changed.

— King Lear

Sorrow so royally in you appears,
That I will deeply put the fashion on.

— Henry IV

FAULT

The fault, dear Brutus, is not in our stars,
But in ourselves, that we are underlings.

— *Julius Caesar*

Condemn the fault and not the actor of it?

— *Measure for Measure*

If sack and sugar be a fault, God help the wicked!

— *Henry IV*

O England! model to thy inward greatness,
Like little body with a mighty heart,
What might'st thou do, that honour would thee do,
Were all thy children kind and natural!
But see thy fault.

— *Henry V*

Every one fault seeming monstrous till
his fellow fault came to match it.

— *As You Like It*

Why, man, he doth bestride the narrow world,
Like a colossus; and we petty men walk under his huge
legs, and peep about to find ourselves dishonourable graves.
Men at some time are masters of their fates:
The fault, dear Brutus, is not in our stars,
But in ourselves, that we are underlings.

— *Julius Caesar*

FEAR

In time we hate that which we often fear.

— Antony and Cleopatra

Fear no more the frown o' the great,
Thou art past the tyrant's stroke:

— Cymbeline

Distill'd
Almost to jelly with the act of fear.

— Hamlet

A largess universal, like the sun
His liberal eye doth give to every one,
Thawing cold fear.

— Henry V

True nobility is exempt from fear.

— Henry VI

Of all the wonders that I yet have heard,
It seems to me most strange that men should fear.

— Julius Caesar

Cuckoo, cuckoo; o, word of fear,
Unpleasing to a married ear!

— Love's Labour's Lost

I know not how,
But I do find it cowardly and vile,
For fear of what might fall, so to prevent
The time of life.

— Julius Caesar

That I may tell pale-hearted fear it lies,
And sleep in spite of thunder.

— *Macbeth*

Bring me no more reports: let them fly all:
Till Birnam wood remove to Dunsinane
I cannot taint with fear.

— *Macbeth*

The weariest and most loathed worldly life
That age, ache, penury, and imprisonment
Can lay on nature, is a paradise
To what we fear of death.

— *Measure for Measure*

Rash-embrac'd despair,
And shuddering fear, and green-ey'd jealousy.

— *The Merchant of Venice*

There is none but he
Whose being I do fear: and, under him
My genius is rebuk'd: as, it is said,
Mark Antony's was by Caesar.

— *Macbeth*

FLESH

O, that this too too solid flesh would melt,
Thaw and resolve itself into a dew.

— Hamlet

Mount, Mount, my soul! thy seat is upon high,
Whist my gross flesh sinks downwards, here to die.

— Richard II

O flesh, flesh, how art thou fishified!

— Romeo and Juliet

Lay her i' the earth;
And from her fair and unpolluted flesh
My violets spring! I tell thee, churlish priest,
A ministering angel shall my sister be,
when thou liest howling.

— Hamlet

On the AIPS
It is reported thou didst eat strange flesh,
Which some did die to look on.

— Antony and Cleopatra

I have more flesh than another man,
and therefore more frailty.

— Henry IV

Thy ignominy sleep with thee in the grave,
But not remember'd in thy epitaph!
What! old acquaintance! could not all this flesh
Keep in a little life? poor Jack, Farewell!
I could have better spar'd better man.

— Henry IV

FLOWERS

When daisies pied and violets blue
And lady — smocks all silver — white
And cuckoo-buds of yellow hue
Do paint the meadows with delight.

— *Love's Labour's Lost*

I know a bank where the wild thyme blows
Where oxslips and the nodding violet grows,
Quite over-canopied with luscious woodbine,
With sweet musk-roses and with eglantine.

— *A Midsummer Night's Dream*

The summer's flowers is to the summer sweet,
Though to itself it only live and die.

— *Sonnet-94*

There's rose-mary, that's for remembrance —
pray you love, remember. And there is
pansies, that's for thoughts.

— *Hamlet*

For you there's rose mary and rue, these keep
Seeming and savor all the winter long.

— *The Winter's Tale*

Thou shalt not lack
The flower that's like thy face, pale primrose, nor
The azur'd harebell, like thy veins.

— *Cymbeline*

FOOD

He hath eaten me out of house and home.

— Henry IV

I am a great eater of beef and I
believe that does harm to my wit.

— Twelfth Night

Who doth ambition shun
And loves to live i' the sun,
Seeking the food he eats,
And pleas'd with what he gets.

— As You Like It

But mice and rats and such small deer
Have been Tom's food for seven long year.

— King Lear

Chewing the food of sweet and bitter fancy.

— As You Like It

Music, mood food
of us that trade in love.

— Antony and Cleopatra

Tut, tut; good enough to toss; food
for powder, food for powder; they'll fill a pit
as well as better: tush, man, mortal men,
mortal men.

— Henry IV

If music be the food of love, play on;
Give me excess of it, that, surfeiting,
The appetite may sicken, and so die,
That strain again! it had a dying fall:

— Twelfth Night

FOOL

What fools these mortals be!

— *A Midsummer Night's Dream*

The triple pillar of the world transform'd
Into a strumpet's fool.

— *Antony and Cleopatra*

We make guilty of our disasters the sun, the moon, and the stars; as if we were villains by necessity, fools by heavenly compulsion.

— *King Lear*

Why should I play the Roman Fool, and die on mine own sword?

— *Macbeth*

Be absolute for death: either death or life
Shall thereby be the sweeter, Reason thus with life:
If I do lose thee, I do lose a thing
That none but fools would keep: a breath thou art
Servile to all the skyey influences.

— *Measure for Measure*

This fellow's wise enough to play the fool,
And to do that well craves a kind of wit.

— *Twelfth Night*

You fools of fortune, trencher-friends time's flies.

— *Timon of Athens*

When we are born we cry that we are come
To this great stage of fools.

— *King Lear*

And my poor fool is hang'd! No, no, no life!
Why should a dog, a horse, a rat, have life,
And thou no breath at all? Thou'lt come no more,
Never, never, never, never, never!
Pray you, undo this button.

— *King Lear*

She never yet was foolish that was fair,
For even her folly help'd her to an heir.

— *Othello*

Thus do I ever make my fool my purse.

— *Othello*

Pretty fool, it stinted and said 'Ay'.

— *Romeo and Juliet*

Relenting fool, and shallow, changing woman!

— *Richard III*

Thus hath the candle sing'd the moth.
O, these deliberate fools!

— *The Merchant of Venice*

What says Quinapalus? 'Better a witty
fool than a foolish wit'.

— *Twelfth Night*

How every fool can play upon the word!

— *The Merchant of Venice*

FORGIVENESS

The quality of mercy is not strained,
It droppeth as the gentle rain from heaven.

— *Merchant of Venice*

No beast so fierce but knows some touch of pity.

— *Richard III*

Sweet mercy is nobility's true badge.

— *Titus Andronicus*

Pray you now, forget and forgive.

— *King Lear*

Come, let's away to prison;
We two alone will sing like birds i' the cage;
When thou dost ask me blessing, I'll kneel down,
And ask for thee forgiveness, and we'll live,
And pray, and sing, and tell old tales, and laugh,
At gilded butterflies, and hear poor rogues,
Talk of court news; and we'll talk with them too,
Who loses, and who wins; who's in, who's out:
And take upon 's the mystery of things,
As if were God's spies; and we'll wear out,
In a wall'd prison, packs and sets of great ones,
That ebb and flow by the moon.

— *King Lear*

FORTUNE

Let us sit and mock the good housewife
fortune from her wheel, that her gifts
may henceforth be bestowed equally.

— As You Like It

O! I am fortune's food.

— Romeo and Juliet

A man that fortune's buffets and rewards
Hast ta'en with equal thanks; and bless'd are those
Whose blood and Judgment are so well co-mingled.
That they are not a pipe for fortune's finger
To sound what stop she please. Give me that man
That is not passion's slave, and I will wear him,
In my heart's core, ay, in my heart of heart,
As I do thee. Something too much of this.

— Hamlet

Fortune is merry,
And in this mood will give us anything.

— Julius Caesar

Disdaining fortune, with his brandish'd steel,
Which smok'd with bloody execution,
Like valour's minion carv'd out his passage.

— Macbeth

The lowest and most dejected thing of fortune.

— King Lear

'What is your parentage?'
'Above my fortune, yet my state is well:
I am a gentleman'.

— Twelfth Night

O! I am fortune's fool.

— *Romeo and Juliet*

For herein Fortune shows herself more kind
That is her custom: it is still her use
To let the wretched man outlive his wealth,
To view with hollow eye and wrinkled brow
An age of poverty.

— *The Merchant of Venice*

If I do prove her haggard,
Though that her jesses were my dear heart-strings,
I'd whistle her off and let her down the wind,
To prey at fortune.

— *Othello*

To be a well-favoured man is the
gift of fortune; but to write and
read comes by nature.

— *Much Ado About Nothing.*

FREE

I would not my unhoused free condition
Put into circumscription and confine
For the sea's worth.

— *Othello*

The moor is of a free and open nature,
That thinks men honest that but seem to be so.

— *Othello*

Thought is free.

— *The Tempest*

When the mind's free,
The body's delicate.

— *King Lear*

Not with such familiar instances,
Nor with such free and friendly conference,
As he hath us'd of old.

— *Julius Caesar*

O Conspiracy!
Sham'st thou to show thy dangerous brow by night,
When evils are most free?

— *Julius Caesar*

We that have free souls, it touches us not;
let the galled jade wince, our withers are
unwrung.

— *Hamlet*

Make mad the guilty, and appal the free,
Confound the ignorant, and amaze, indeed.
The very faculties of eyes and ears.

— *Hamlet*

FRIENDSHIP

Most friendship is feigning, most loving mere folly.

— As You Like It

Those friends thou hast, and their adoption tried,
Grapple them to thy soul with hoops of steel.

— Hamlet

A friend should bear his friend's infirmities
But Brutus makes mine greater than they are.

— Julius Caesar

Those friends thou hast, and their adoption tried
Grapple them to thy soul with hoops of steel;
But do not dull they palm with entertainment,
Of each news-hatched, unfledged comrade.

— Hamlet

To me, fair friend, you never can be old.

— Sonnet-104

For when did friendship take
A breed for barren metal of his friend?

— The Merchant of Venice

Friendship is constant in all other things
Save in the office and affairs of love.

— Much Ado About Nothing

The gods to-day stand friendly, that we may,
Lovers in peace on our days to age!

— Julius Caesar

The great man down, you mark his favourite flies;
The poor advanc'd makes friends of enemies.

— Hamlet

A good plot, good friends, and full of expectation; an excellent plot, very good friends.

— Henry IV

I had rather have
Such men my friends than enemies.

— Julius Caesar

Call you that backing of your friends?
A plague upon such backing! give me them that will face me.

— Henry IV

You fools of fortune, trencher-friends time's flies.

— Timon of Athens

I count myself in nothing else so happy
As in a soul remembering my good friends.

— Richard II

Brutus, I do observe you now of late:
I have not from your eyes that gentleness
And show of love as I was wont to have:
You bear too stubborn and too strange a hand
Over your friend that loves you.

— Julius Caesar

A friendly eye could never see such faults.

— Julius Caesar

This passion, and the death of a dear friend,
Would go near to make a man look sad.

— A Midsummer Night's Dream

He was my friend, faithful and just to me:
But Brutus says he was ambitious:
And Brutus is an honourable man.

— Julius Caesar

The world is not thy friend, nor the world's law.

— *Romeo* and *Juliet*

Yet the first bringer of unwelcome news
Hath but a losing office, and his tongue,
Sounds ever after as a sullen bell,
Remember'd knolling a departed friend.

— *Henry IV*

Good Hamlet, cast thy nighted colour off,
And let thine eye look like a friend on Denmark.

— *Hamlet*

He that wants money, means, and
Content is without three good friends.

— *As You Like It*

GAMBLING

In my school days, when I had lost one shaft,
I shot his fellow of the self-same flight
The self-same way, with more advised watch,
To find the other forth; and by advent'ring both
I oft found both.

— *Merchant of Venice*

Thy bones are marrowless, thy blood is cold;
Thou hast no speculation is those eyes
which thou dost glare with.

— *Macbeth*

GARDEN

O! that this too too solid flesh would melt,
Thaw, and resolve itself into a dew;
Or that the Everlasting had not fix'd
His canon 'gainst self-slaughter! O God! O God!
How weary, stale, flat, and unprofitable
Seem to me all the uses of this world.
Fie on't! o Fie! 'tis an unweeded garden,
That grows to seed; things rank and gross in nature,
Possess it merely.

— *Hamlet*

Old Adam's likeness, set to dress this garden.

— *Richard II*

GHOST

The time has been
That when the brains were out, the man would die,
And there an end; but now they rise again
with twenty mortal murders on their crowns.

— Macbeth

I am thy father's spirit
Doom'd for a certain time to walk the night.

— Hamlet

Alas! poor ghost.

— Hamlet

Vex not his ghost; O! let him pass; he hates him.
That would upon the rack of this tough world,
Stretch him out longer.

— King Lear

That affable familiar ghost
which nightly gulls him with intelligence.

— Sonnet-86

It is an honest ghost, that let me tell you.

— Hamlet

There needs no ghost, my lord, come from
the grave,
To tell us this.

— Hamlet

GIANT

Oh, it is excellent
To have giant's strength; but it is tyrannous
To use it like a giant.

— *Measure for Measure*

Dar'st thou die?
The sense of death is most in apprehension,
And the poor beetle, that we tread upon,
In corporeal sufferance finds a pang as great
As when a giant dies.

— *Measure for Measure*

Those he commands move only in command,
Nothing in love; now does he feel his title
Hang loose about him, like a giant's robe
Upon a dwarfish thief.

— *Macbeth*

And in such indexes, although small pricks
To their subsequent volumes, there is seen
The baby figure of the giant mass
Of things to come at large.

— *Troilus and Cressida*

This wimpled, whinning, purbling, wayward boy,
This senior-junior, giant-dwarf, Dan Cupid;
Regent of love rhymes, lord of folded arms,
The anointed sovereign of sighs and groans,
Liege of all loiterers and malcontents.

— *Love's Labour's Lost*

GLORY

Say, wulsey, that once trod the ways of glory,
And sounded all the depths and shoals of honour,
Found thee a way, out of his wrack, to rise in;
A sure and safe one, though thy master miss'd it.

— *Henry VIII*

No glory lives behind the back of such.

— *Much Ado About Nothing*

So doth the greater glory dim the less:
A substitute shines brightly as a king
Until a king be by, and then his state
Empties itself, as doth an inland brook
Into the main of waters.

— *The Merchant of Venice*

Is not the king's name twenty thousand names?
Arm, arm, my name! A puny subject strikes
At thy great glory.

— *Richard II*

Like madness is the glory of this life.

— *Timon of Athens*

O! the fierce wretchedness that glory brings us.

— *Timon of Athens*

GO

Whither wilt thou lead me? Speak;
I'll go no further.

— Hamlet

Stand not upon the order of your going,
But go at once.

— Macbeth

Then sigh not so,
But let them go,
And be you blithe and bonny,
Converting all your sounds of woe
Into Hey nonny, nonny.

— Much Ado About Nothing

The king shall be contented; must he lose
The name of king? O' God's name, let it go.

— Richard II

You know that love
Will creep in service where it cannot go.

— Two Gentlemen of Verona

I go, and it is done; the bell invites me.

— Macbeth

GOD

It holds his estimate and dignity
As well wherein 'tis precious of itself
As in the prizer. 'Tis mad idolatry
To make the service greater than the god.

— *Troilus and Cressida*

Do not swear at all;
Or, if thou wilt, swear by thy gracious self,
Which is the god of my idolatry.

— *Romeo and Juliet*

God save the king! will no man say amen?
Am I both priest and clerk? well then amen.

— *Richard II*

Well, God's a good man.

— *Much Ado About Nothing*

Here will be an old abusing of God's
Patience, and the king's English.

— *The Merry Wives of Windsor*

Why, then, God's soldier be he!
Had I as many sons as I have hairs
I would not wish them to a fairer death.

— *Macbeth*

God made him, and therefore let him pass for a man.

— *The Merchant of Venice*

In the great hand of God I stand, and thence
Against the undivulg'd pretence I fight
of treasonous malice.

— *Macbeth*

Had I but serv'd my God with half the zeal
I serv'd my king, he would not in mine age
Have left me naked to mine enemies.

— *Henry VIII*

O God of battles! steel my soldiers' hearts;

— *Henry V*

Let all the ends thou aim'st at be thy country's,
Thy God's, and truth's.

— *Henry VIII*

Follow your spirit; and, upon this charge
Cry 'God for Harry! England and Saint George!'

— *Henry V*

God hath given you one face, and you
make yourselves another.

— *Hamlet*

If sack and sugar be a fault, God help the wicked!

— *Henry IV*

GOODNESS

There is some soul of goodness in things evil,
Would men observingly distil it out.

— Henry V

Virtue is bold, and goodness never fearful.

— Measure for Measure

Wisdom and goodness to the vile seem vile;
Fiths savour but themselves.

— King Lear

Are you good men and true?

— Much Ado About Nothing

Against ill chances men are ever merry,
But heaviness foreruns the good event.

— Henry IV

Whate'er you think, good words, I think, were best.

— King John

'Tis well said again;
And 'tis a kind of good deed to say well:
And yet words are no deeds,

— Henry VIII

These late eclipses in the sun and moon
portend no good to us.

— King Lear

He, only, in a general honest thought
And common good to all, made one of them.
His life was gentle, and the elements.

So mix'd in him that Nature might stand up
And say to all the world, 'This was a man'!

— *Julius Caesar*

Though music oft hath such a charm
To make bad good, and good provoke to harm.

— *Measure for Measure*

If to do were as easy as to know
what were good to do, chapels had been
churches, and poor men's cottages princes'
palaces.

— *The Merchant of Venice*

Yet this shall I ne'er know, but live in doubt,
Till my bad angel fire my good one out.

— *Sonnet-144*

Time hath, my lord, a wallet at his back,
wherein he puts alms for oblivion,
A great-siz'd monster of ingratitudes;
Those scraps are good deeds past; which are devour'd
As fast as they are made, forgot as soon
as done.

— *Troilus and Cressida*

It was always yet the trick of our
English nation, if they have a good thing, to
make it too common.

— *Henry IV*

Pour out the pack of matter to mine ear,
The good and bad together.

— *Antony and Cleopatra*

It is a good divine that follows his own instructions;
I can easier teach twenty what were good
to be done, than be one of the twenty to
follow mine own teaching.

— *The Merchant of Venice*

Though music oft hath such a charm
To make bad good, and good provoke to harm.

— *Measure for Measure*

How far that little candle throws his beams!
So shines a good deed in a naughty world.

— *The Merchant of Venice*

I will roar, that I will do any man's
heart good to hear me.

— *A Midsummer Night's Dream*

Well, God's a good man.

— *Much Ado About Nothing*

Our doubts are traitors,
And make us lose the good we oft might win,
By fearing to attempt.

— *Measure for Measure*

The hand that hath made you fair hath made you good.

— *Measure for Measure*

We, ignorant of ourselves,
Beg often our own harms, which the wise powers,
Deny us for our good; so find we profit
By losing of our prayers.

— *Antony and Cleopatra*

I earn that I eat, get that I wear, owe
no man hate, envy no man's happiness,
glad of other men's good, content with
my harm.

— *As You Like It*

It is not, nor it cannot come to good;
But break, my heart, for I must hold my tongue!

— *Hamlet*

There is nothing either good or bad, but
thinking makes it so.

— *Hamlet.*

There's nothing ill can dwell in such a temple;
If the ill spirit have so fair a house,
Good things will strive to dwell with 't.

— *The Tempest*

Though it be honest, it is never good
To bring bad news; give to a gracious message
A host of tongues, but let ill tidings tell
Themselves when they be felt.

— *Antony and Cleopatra*

GREATNESS

Why, man, he doth be stride the narrow world
Like a colossus, and we petty men
Walk under his huge legs and peep about
To find ourselves dishonourable graves.

— Julius Caesar

But be not afraid of greatness: some are born great, some achieve greatness and some have greatness thrust upon 'em.

— Twelfth Night

....Some are born great, some achieve greatness and some have greatness thrust upon 'em.

— Twelfth Night

Nice customs curtesy to great kings.

— Henry V

I would not be a queen
For all the world.

— Henry VIII

For God's sake, let us sit upon the ground
And tell sad stories of the death of the kings.

— Richard II

Now is the winter of our discontent
Made glorious summer by this sun of york.

— Richard III

And what have king that privates have not too,
Save ceremony, save general ceremony.

— Henry V

Uneasy lies the head that wears a crown.

— Henry IV

The soul and body rive not more in parting
Than greatness going off.

— Antony and Cleopatra

His greatness weigh'd, his will is not his own,
For he himself is subject to his birth;
He may not, as unvalu'd persons do,
Carve for himself, for on his choice depends
The safety and the health of the whole State.

— Hamlet

Die two months ago, and not forgotten yet?
Then there's hope a great man's memory
may outlive his life half a year; but,
by'r lady, he must build churches then.

— Hamlet

Antony
Shall be brought drunken forth, and I shall see
Some squeaking Cleopatra boy my greatness
I' the posture of a whore.

— Antony and Cleopatra

Greatness knows itself.

— Henry IV

O! that I were as great
As is my grief, or lesser than my name,
or that I could forget what I have been,
or not remember what I must be now.

— Richard II

Great men may jest with saints; 'tis wit in them,
But, in the less foul profanation.

— Measure for Measure

O England! model to thy inward greatness,
Like little body with a mighty heart,
What might'st thou do, that honour would thee do,

Were all thy children kind and natural!
But see thy fault!

— *Henry V*

'Brutus' will start a spirit as soon as 'Caesar'.
Now in the names of all the gods at once,
Upon what meat doth this our Caesar feed,
That he is grown so great?

— *Julius Caesar*

Wrest once the law to your authority:
To do a great right, do a little wrong.

— *The Merchant of Venice*

Rightly to be great
Is not to stir without great argument,
But greatly to find quarrel in a straw
when honour's at the stake.

— *Hamlet*

GRIEF

What! man; ne'er pull your hat upon your brows;
Give sorrow words: the grief that does not speak
Whispers the o'er-fraught heart, and bids it break.

— Macbeth

Well, every one can master a grief
but he that has it.

— Much Ado About Nothing

My particular grief
Is of so flood-gate and o'er bearing nature
That it engluts and swallows other sorrows
And it is still itself.

— Othello

Patch grief with proverbs.

— Much Ado About Nothing

Boast of nothing else
But that I was a journeyman to grief?

— Richard II

O! that I were as great
As is my grief, or lesser than my name,
Or that I could forget what I have been,
Or not remember what I must be now.

— Richard II

She sat like patience on a monument,
Smiling at grief.

— Twelfth Night

What's gone, and what's past help
Should be past grief.

— The Winter's Tale

His flaw'd heart,
Alack! too weak the conflict to support;
'Twixt two extremes of passion, joy and grief,
Burst smilingly.

— King Lear

You see me here, you gods, a poor old man,
As full of grief as age; wretched in both!

— King Lear

Verily,
I swear 'tis better to be lowly born,
And range with humble livers in content,
Than to be perk'd up, in a glist'ring grief,
And wear a golden sorrow.

— Henry VIII

O Cassius! I am sick of many griefs.

— Julius Caesar

Grief fills the room up of my absent child,
Lies in his bed, walks up and down with me,
Puts on his pretty looks, repeats his words,
Remembers me of all his gracious parts,
Stuffs out his vacant garments with his form.

— King John

Is there no pity sitting in the clouds,
That sees into the bottom of my grief?

— Romeo and Juliet

You may my glories and my state depose,
But not my griefs; still am I king of those.

— Richard II

But to persever
In obstinate condolement is a course
Of impious stubbornness; 'tis unmanly grief;

It shows a will most incorrect to heaven,
A heart unfortified, a mind impatient.

— *Hamlet*

A plague of sighing and grief! It
blows a man up like a bladder.

— *Henry IV*

HATE

My only love sprung from my only hate!

— Romeo and Juliet

Sweet love, I see, changing his property,
Turns to the sourest and most deadly hate.

— Richard II

An honourable murderer, if you will;
For nought did I in hate, but all in honour.

— Othello

I do hate him as I do hell-pains.

— Othello

How like a fawning publican he looks!
I hate him for he is a Christian :

— The Merchant of Venice

Love thyself last: cherish those hearts that hate thee;
Corruption wins not more than honesty.

— Henry VIII

I earn that I eat, get that I wear, owe
no man hate, envy no man's happiness,
glad of other men's good, content with
my harm.

— As You Like It

HAIR

His hair is of a good colour.

— As You Like It

Yea, beg a hair of him for memory,
And, dying, mention it within their wills,
Bequeathing it as a rich legacy
Unto their issue.

— Julius Caesar

Had I as many sons as I have hairs,
I would not wish them to a fairer death.

— Macbeth

She has brown hair, and speaks small like a woman.

— The Merry Wives of Windsor

Had all his hairs been lives, my great revenge.
Had stomach for them all.

— Othello

Then hadst thou had an excellent head of hair.

— Twelfth Night

Now Jove, in his next commodity of
hair, send thee a beard.

— Twelfth Night

HANDS

All the perfumes of Arabia will not
sweeten this little hand.

— Macbeth

See! how she leans her cheek upon her hand!
O, that I were a glove upon that hand,
That I might touch that cheek!

— Romeo and Juliet

Will all great Neptune's ocean wash this blood
Clean from my hand? No, this my hand will rather,
The multitudinous seas incarnadine,
Making the green one red.

— Macbeth

I'll follow thee and make a heaven of a hell,
To die upon the hand I love so well.

— A Midsummer Night's Dream

The Thane of Fife had a wife: where is
she now? what! will these hands ne'er be clean?

— Macbeth

The hand that hath made you fair hath
made you good.

— Measure for Measure

The hearts of old gave hands,
But our new heraldry is hands not hearts.

— Othello

That it went hand in hand even with the vow
I made to her in marriage.

— Hamlet

My play fellow, your hand; this kingly seal
And plighter of high hearts.

— Antony and Cleopatra

Brutus, I do observe you now of late;
I have not from your eyes that gentleness
And show of love as I was wont to have:
You bear too stubborn and too strange a hand
over your friend that loves you.

— Julius Caesar

The eye of man hath not heard, the ear
of man hath not seen, man's hand is
not able to taste, his tongue to conceive,
nor his heart to report, what my
dream was.

— A Midsummer Night's Dream

My heart is turned to stone; I strike it,
and it hurts my hand.

— Othello

FERDINAND : Here's my hand
MIRANDA : And mine, with my heart in't.

— The Tempest

Will all great Neptune's ocean wash this blood
Clean from my hand? No, this my hand will rather
The multitudinous seas incarnadine,
making the green one red.

— Macbeth

Keep thy foot out of brothels, thy hand out
of plackets, thy pen from lenders' book,
and defy the foul fiend.

— King Lear

Is this a daggar which I see before me,
The handle toward my hand? Come, let me clutch thee:

— Macbeth

The hand of little employment hath the
daintier sense.

— *Hamlet*

There is gold, and here
My bluest veins to kiss; a hand that kings
Have lipp'd and trembled kissing.

— *Antony and Cleopatra*

At hand, quoth pick-purse.

— *Henry IV*

Have you not a moist eye, a dry hand,
a yellow cheek, a white beard, a
decreasing leg, an increasing bell?

— *Henry IV*

That handkerchief
Did an Egyptian to my mother give.

— *Othello*

With mine own tears I wash away my balm,
with mine own hands I give away my crown.

— *Richard II*

I weep for Joy
To stand upon my kingdom once again.
Dear earth, I do salute thee with my hand,
Though rebels wound thee with their horses' hoofs.

— *Richard II*

O! that her hand,
In those comparison all whites are ink,
Writing their own reproach; to whose soft seizure
The cygnet's down is harsh, and spirit of sense
Hard as the palm of ploughman.

— *Troilus and Cressida*

Three crabbed mouths had sour'd
themselves to death,
Ere I could make thee open thy white hand
And clap thyself my love.

— *The Winter's Tale*

I think we do know the sweet Roman hand.

— Twelfth Night

O heaven! that such companions thou'dst unfold,
And put in every honest hand a whip
To lash the rascals naked through the world,
Even from the east to the west.

— Othello

O! who can hold a fire in his hand
By thinking on the frosty caucasus?
Or cloy the hungry edge to appetite,
By bare imagination of a feast?
Or wallow naked in December snow
By thinking on fantastic summer's heat?

— Richard II

Let each man render me his bloody hand
First, Marcus Brutus, will I shake with you.

— Julius Caesar

In the great hand of God I stand, and thence
Against the undivulg'd pretence I fight
of treason malice.

— Macbeth

So every bondman in his own hand bears
The power to cancel his captivity.

— Julius Caesar

HAPPINESS

O, how bitter a thing it is to look into
happiness through another man's eyes!

— As You Like It

O wonderful, wonderful, and most wonderful! and yet
again wonderful and after that, out of all whooping!

— As You Like It

If it be my luck, So; if not, happy man
be his dole!

— The Merry Wives of Windsor

Silence is the perfectect heralds of Joy: I
were but little happy, if I could say how
much.

— Much Ado About Nothing

But earthlier happy is the rose distill'd,
Than that which withering on the virgin thorn
Grows, lives, and dies, in single blessedness.

— A Midsummer Night's Dream

If it were how to die,
'Twere now to be most happy, for I fear
My soul hath her content so absolute
That not another comfort like to this
succeeds in unknown fate.

— Othello

HEAD

The head is not more native to the heart.

— *Hamlet*

He is dead and gone, lady,
He is dead and gone,
At his head a grass-green turf;
At his heels a stone.

— *Hamlet*

The sea, with such a storm as his bare head
In hell-black night endur'd, would have buoy'd up,
And quench'd the stelled fires.

— *King Lear*

The hedge-sparrow fed the Cuckoo so long.
That it had it head bit off by it young.

— *King Lear*

My deeds upon my head! I crave the law.

— *The Merchant of Venice*

Thou cutt'st my head off with a golden axe.

— *Romeo and Juliet*

Now does my project gather to a head.

— *The Tempest*

Who wears his wit in his belly,
and his guts in his head.

— *Troilus and Cressida*

HEART

What stronger breast plate than a heart untainted!

— Henry VI

'Tis sweating labour
To bear such idleness so near the heart
As Cleopatra this.

— Antony and Cleopatra

O tiger's heart wrapp'd in a woman's hide!

— Henry VI

She bears a duke's revenues on her back,
And in her heart she scorns our poverty.

— Henry VI

A goodly apple rotten at the heart.
O, what a goodly outside falsehood hath!

— The Merchant of Venice

But I will wear my heart upon my sleeve,
For daws to peck at: I am not what I am.

— Othello

The eye of man hath not heard, the
ear of man hath not seen, man's
hand is not able to taste, his tongue
to conceive, nor his heart to report,
what my dream was.

— A Midsummer Night's Dream

Show his eyes, and grieve his heart;
Come like shadows, so depart!

— Macbeth

I will roar, that I will do any
man's heart good to hear me.

— A Midsummer Night's Dream

Away, and mock the time with fairest show:
False face must hide what the false heart doth know.

— *Macbeth*

His flaw'd heart, —
Alack! too weak the conflict to support;
'Twixt two extremes of passion, joy and grief,
Burst smilingly.

— *King Lear*

You are my true and honourable wife,
As dear to me as are the ruddy drops
That visit my sad heart.

— *Julius Caesar*

But thou wouldst not think how
ill all's here about my heart.

— *Hamlet*

O England! model to thy inward greatness,
Like little body with a mighty heart,
What might'st thou do, that honour would thee do,
were all thy children kind and natural!
But see thy fault!

— *Henry V*

My heart is turned to stone; I strike
it, and it hurts my hand.

— *Othello*

There is no woman's sides
Can bide the beating of so strong a passion,
As love doth give my heart; no woman's heart.
So big, to hold so much; they lack retention.

— *Twelfth Night*

Jog on, Jog on the foot-path way,
And merrily hent the stile-a;
A merry heart goes all the day,
Your sad tires in a mile-a.

— *The Winter's Tale*

Ah, do not, when my heart hath 'scap'd this sorrow,
Come in the rearward of a conquer'd woe;
Give not a windy night a rainy morrow,
To linger out a purpos'd overthrow.

— *Sonnet-90*

The very firstlings of my heart shall be
The firstlings of my hand.

— *Macbeth*

Tell me where is fancy bred,
or in the heart or in the head?
How begot, how nourished?
Reply, reply.

— *The Merchant of Venice*

O Hamlet! thou hast cleft my heart in twain.

— *Hamlet*

Now cracks a noble heart. Good night,
Sweet Prince
And flights of angels sing thee to thy rest!

— *Hamlet*

The kingly crowned head, the vigilant eye,
The Counsellor heart, the arm our soldier,
Our steed the leg, the tongue our trumpeter.

— *Coriolanus*

Prosperity's the very bond of love,
whose fresh complexion and whose heart together.
Affliction alters.

— *The Winter's Tale*

What! man: ne'er full your hat upon your brows:
Give sorrow words; the grief that does not speak
Whispers the o'er-fraught heart, and bids it break.

— *Macbeth*

I would not have such a heart in
my bosom for the dignity of the whole body.

— *Macbeth*

HEROES

He was a man, take him for all in all.
I shall not look upon his like again.

— Hamlet

This was the noblest Roman of them all.

— Julius Caesar

His life was gentle, and the elements
So mixed in him that Nature might stand up
And say to all the world, "This was a man."

-- Julius Caesar

HIDE

O tiger's heart wrapp'd in a woman's hide!

— Henry VI

Thou wear a lion's hide! doff it for shame,
And hang a calf's-skin on those recreant limbs!

— King John

Is it a world to hide virtues in?

— Twelfth Night

Round-hoof'd, short-Jointed, fetlocks shag and long,
Broad breast, full eye, small head and nostril wide,
High crest, short ears, straight legs and passing strong,
Thine mane, thick-tail, broad buttock, tender hide:
Look, what a horse should have he did not lack,
Save a proud rider on so proud a back.

— Venus and Adonis

HIGH POSITION

Now is the winter of our discontent
Made glorious summer by this sun of york.

— Richard III

I would not be a queen
For all the world.

— Henry VIII

For God's sake, let us sit upon the ground
And tell sad stories of the death of kings.

— Richard II

And what have kings that privates have not too,
Save ceremony, save general ceremony.

— Henry V

Uneasy lies the head that wears a crown.

— Henry IV

Nice customs curtsey to great kings.

— Henry V

HILL

These high wild hills and rough uneven ways
Draw out our miles and make them wearisome.

— *Richard II*

Pillicock sat on pillicock-hill;
Halloo, halloo, loo, loo!

— *King Lear*

Wherein of antres vast and desarts idle,
Rough quarries, rocks and hills whose heads touch heaven,
It was my hint to speak, such was the process,

— *Othello*

HOME

He hath eaten me out of house and home.

— Henry IV

Hence! home, you idle creatures, get you home:
Is this a holiday?

— Julius Caesar

Thou hast never in thy life
Show'd thy dear mother any courtesy;
When she — poor hen! fond of no second brood-
Has cluck'd thee to the wars, and safely home,
Loaden with honour.

— Coriolanus

Ay, now am I in Arden; the more fool,
I When I was at home I wan in
a better place; but travellers must be content.

— As You Like It

Fear no more the heat o' the sun,
Nor the furious winter's rages;
Thou thy worldly task hast done,
Home art gone and ta'en thy wages:
Golden lads and girls all must,
As chimney-sweepers, come to dust.

— Cymbeline

HONESTY

No legacy is so rich as honesty.

— *All's Well That Ends Well*

To be honest, as this word goes, is to be
one man picked out of ten thousand.

— *Hamlet*

Men should be what they seem.

— *Othello*

Every man has his fault, and honesty is his.

— *Timon of Athens*

Take note, take note, o world!
To be direct and honest is not safe.

— *Othello*

Thus may we gather honey from the weed,
And make a moral of the devil himself.

— *King Henry V*

As the honey of Hybla, my old lad of the castle.

— *King Henry IV*

Being daily swallow'd by men's eyes,
They surfeited with honey and began
To loathe the taste of sweetness, where of a little,
More than a little is by much too much.
So, when he had occasion to be seen,
He was but as the Cuckoo is in June,
Heard, not regarded.

— *King Henry IV*

HONOUR

By heaven, methinks it were an easy leap
To pluck bright honour from the pale-faced moon,
Or dive into the bottom of the deep,
Where fathom-line could never touch the ground,
And pluck up drowned honour by the locks.

— Henry IV

Well, honour is the subject of my story.
I cannot tell what you and other men
Think of this life: but, for my single self,
I had as lief not be as live to be
In awe of such a thing as I myself.

— Julius Caesar

Mine honour is my life.

— Richard II

He lives in fame that died in virtue's cause.

— Titus Andronicus

How far that little candle throws his beams!
So shines a good deed in a naughty world.

— Merchant of Venice

After my death I wish no other herald.
No other speaker of my living actions,
To keep mine honour from corruption,
Than such an honest chronicler as Griffith.

— Henry VIII

Well, honour is the subject of my story,
I cannot tell what you and other men
Think of this life: but, for my single self,

I had as lief not be as live to be
I awe of such a thing as I myself.

— *Julius Caesar*

Perseverance, dear my lord,
Keeps honour bright; to have done, is to hang
Quite out of fashion, like a rusty mail
In monumental mockery.

— *Troilus and Cressida*

An honourable murderer, if you will;
For nought did I in hate, but all in honour.

— *Othello*

Thou art a fellow of a good respect;
Thy life hath had some smatch of honour in it.

— *Julius Caesar*

Set honour in one eye and death i' the other,
And I will look on both indifferently.

— *Julius Caesar*

Those about her
From her shall read the perfect ways of honour.

— *King Henry VIII*

If he fall in, good-night! or sink or swim;
Send danger from the east unto the west,
So honour cross it from the north to south,
And let them grapple: O! the blood more stirs
To rouse a lion than to start a hare.

— *King Henry IV*

So well thy words become thee as thy wounds;
They smack of honour both.

— *Macbeth*

A Daniel come to judgment! yea, a Daniel!
O wise young Judge, how I do honour thee!

— *The Merchant of Venice*

Let none presume
To wear an undeserved dignity.

O! that estates, degrees, and offices
were not deriv'd corruptly, and that clear honour
were purchased by the merit of the wearer!

— *The Merchant of Venice*

Let's teach ourselves that honourable stop,
Not to outsport discretion.

— *Othello*

And as the sun breaks through the darkest clouds,
So honour peereth in the meanest habit.

— *The Taming of the Shrew*

For honour travels in a strait so narrow
Where one but goes abreast.

— *Troilus and Cressida*

I am not coveteous for gold,
But if it be a sin to covet honour
I am the most offending soul, alive.

— *King Henry V*

Let us make an honourable retreat;
though not with bag and baggage, yet
with scrip and scrippage.

— *As You Like It*

If we are mark'd to die, we are enow
To do our country loss; and if to live,
The fewer men, the greater share of honour.

— *King Henry V*

The painful warrior famoused for fight,
After a thousand victories once foil'd,
Is from the book of honour razed quite,
And all the rest forgot for which he toil'd.

— *Sonnet-25*

As he was valiant, I honour him: but,
as he was ambitious, I slew him.

— *Julius Caesar*

I like not such grinning honour as Sir Walter hath; give me life: which if I can save, so; if not, honour comes unlooked for, and there's an end.

— *King Henry IV*

HOPE

True hope is swift, and flies with swallow's wings
Kings it makes gods, and meaner creature kings.

— Richard III

Nay, do not think I flatter;
For what advancement may I hope from thee,
That no revenue hast, but thy good spirits?

— Hamlet

And be these juggling fiends no more believ'd,
That palter with us in a double sense:
That keep the word of promise to our ear,
And break it to our hope.

— Macbeth

Men that hazard all
Do it in hope of fair advantages:
A golden mind stoops not to shows of dross.

— The Merchant of Venice

Alas! why gnaw you so your nether lip?
Some bloody passion shakes your very frame;
These are portents, but yet, I hope, I hope,
They do not point on me.

— Othello

HYPOCRISY

To beguile the time,
Look like the time...
....look like the innocent flower,
But be the serpent under't

— *Macbeth*

The devil can cite scripture for his purpose.
An evil soul, producing holy witness,
Is like a villain with a smiling cheek,
A goodly apple rotten at the heart;
O, what a goodly outside falsehood hath?

— *Merchant of Venice*

With devotion's usage
And pious action we do sugar o'er
The devil himself.

— *Hamlet*

I know a trick worth two of that.

— *Henry IV*

Friends, Romans, countrymen, lend me your ears;
I come to bury Caesar, not to praise him.

— *Julius Caesar*

Now step I forth to whip hypocrisy.

— *Love's Labour's Lost*

IGNORANCE

There is no ignorance but darkness.

— Twelfth Night

A very superficial, ignorant, unweighing fellow.

— Measure for Measure

We, ignorant of ourselves,
Beg often our own harms, which the wise powers,
Deny us for our good; so find we profit
By losing of our prayers.

— Antony and Cleopatra

He would drown the stage with tears,
And cleave the general ear with horrid speech,
Make mad the guilty, and appal the free,
Confound the ignorant, and amaze, indeed,
The very faculties of eyes and ears.

— Hamlet

Merciful Heaven!
Thou rather with thy sharp and sulphurous bolt,
Split'st the unwedgeable and gnarled oak
Than the soft myrtle; but man, proud man,
Drest in a little brief authority,
Most ignorant of what he's most assur'd,
His glassy essence, like an angry ape,
Plays such fantastic tricks before high heaven,
As make the angels weep.

— Measure for Measure

IMAGINATION

The lunatic, the lover, and the poet
Are of imagination all compact:

— A Midsummer Night's Dream

There is nothing either good or bad but
thinking makes it so.

— Hamlet

They wish was father, Harry, to that thought.

— Henry IV

The best in this kind are but shadows,
and the worst are no worse, if
imagination amend them.

— A Midsummer Night's Dream

The idea of her life shall sweetly creep
Into his study of imagination,
And every lovely organ of her life
Shall come apparell'd in more precious habit,
More moving-delicate, and full of life
Into the eye and prospect of his soul.

— Much Ado About Nothing

I am very proud, revengeful, ambitious;
with more offences at my beck, than I
have thoughts to put them in, imagination
to give them shape, or time to
act them in. What should such fellows
as I do crawling between heaven and earth?

— Hamlet

IMMORTALITY

I do not set my life at a pin's fee;
And, for my soul, what can it do to that,
Being a thing immortal as itself?

— *Hamlet*

His biting is immortal; those that do
die of it do seldom or never recover.

— *Antony* and *Cleopatra*

I have
Immortal longings in me.

— *Antony* and *Cleopatra*

Look, here's the warrant, Claudio, for thy death:
'Tis now dead midnight, and by eight to-morrow,
Thou must be made immortal.

— *Measure for Measure*

Reputation, reputation, reputation! O!
I have lost my reputation. I have lost
the immortal part of myself, and what
remains is bestial, my reputation, Iago,
my reputation!

— *Othello*

INGRATITUDE

Et tu Brute? Then fall, Caesar!

— *Julius Caesar*

How sharper than a serpent's tooth it is
To have a thankless child!

— *King Lear*

Freeze, Freeze, thou bitter sky,
Thou dost not bite so high
As benefits forgot.

— *As You Like It*

Blow, blow, thou winter wind,
Thou art not so unkind
As man's ingratitude:
Thy tooth is not so keen,
Because thou art not seen,
Although thy breath be rude,

— *As You Like It*

This was the most unkindest cut of all;
For when the noble Caesar saw him stab,
Ingratitude, more strong than traitors' arms,
Quite vanquish'd him: then burst his mighty heart.

— *Julius Caesar*

Ingratitude, thou marble-hearted fiend,
More hideous, when thou show'st thee in a child,
Than the sea-monster.

— *King Lear*

JEALOUSY

O, beware, my lord, of Jealousy;
It is the green-eyed monster which doth mock
The meat it feeds on.

— *Othello*

Trifles light as air
Are to the jealous confirmation strong
As proofs of holy writ.

— *Othello*

Rash embrac'd despair,
And shuddering fear, and green-ey'd Jealousy.

— *The Merchant of Venice*

Think'st thou I'd make a life of jealousy,
To follow still the changes of the moon
with fresh suspicions? No; to be once in doubt
Is once to be resolved.

— *Othello*

So full of artless jealousy is guilt,
It spills itself in fearing to be spilt.

— *Hamlet*

But Jealous souls will not be answer'd so;
They are not ever jealous for the cause,
But Jealous for they are Jealous.

— *Othello*

'Tis almost morning: I would have thee gone;
And yet no further than a wanton's bird,
Who lets it hop a little from her hand,

Like a poor prisoner in his twisted gyves,
And with a silk thread plucks it back again,
So loving-Jealous of his liberty.

— *Romeo and Juliet*

JEST

Alas, poor yorick! I knew him, Horatio; a
fellow of infinite jest, of most excellent fancy.

— *Hamlet*

A jest's prosperity lies in the ear
of him that hears it, never in the tongue
of him that makes it.

— *Love's Labour's Lost*

Great men may jest with saints; 'tis wit in them,
But, in the less foul profanation.

— *Measure for Measure*

It would be argument for a week,
laugher for a month, and a good jest
for ever.

— *King Henry IV*

A jest's prosperity lies in the ear
of him that hears it, never in the tongue
of him that makes it.

— *Love's Labour's Lost*

Nature hath fram'd strange fellows in her time;
Some that will evermore peep through their eyes
And laugh like parrots at a bagpiper:
And other of such vinegar aspect
That they'll not show their teeth in way of smile,
Though Nestor Swear the Jest be laughable.

— *The Merchant of Venice*

JEW

Still have I borne it with a patient shrug,
For sufferance is the badge of all our tribe;
You call me misbeliever, cut-throat dog,
And spit upon my jewish gaberdine.

— *Merchant of Venice*

Hath not a Jew eyes? hath not a Jew hands,
organs... fed with the same food, hurt
with the same weapons.... If you prick us,
do we not bleed? If you tickle us do we
not laugh? If you poison us, do we not
die? and if you wrong us, shall we not
revenge?

— *Merchant of Venice*

I am a Jew else; an Ebrew Jew.

— *King Henry IV*

I thank thee, Jew, for teaching me that word.

— *The Merchant of Venice*

A second Daniel, a Daniel, Jew!
Now, infidel, I have thee on the hip.

— *The Merchant of Venice*

Then must the Jew be merciful.

— *The Merchant of Venice*

JEWEL

Win her with gifts, if she respect no words
Dumb Jewels often, in their silent kind
more quick than words, do move a woman's mind.

— *Two Gentlemen of Verona*

From the east to western Ind,
No Jewel is like Rosalind.

— *As You Like It*

O! she doth teach the torches to burn bright.
It seems she hangs upon the cheek of night
Like a rich jewel in an Ethiop's ear;
Beauty too rich for use, for earth too dear.

— *Romeo and Juliet*

Like stones of worth they thinly placed are,
Or captain jewels in the carconet.

— *Sonnet-52*

Mine eternal Jewel,
Given to the common enemy of man.

— *Macbeth*

Sweet are the uses of adversity,
which like the toad, ugly and venomous,
wears yet a precious jewel in his head;

— *As You Like It*

JOY

For bonny sweet Robin is all my joy.

— Hamlet

His flaw'd heart, —
Alack! too weak the conflict to support;
'Twixt two extremes of passion, joy and grief
Burst smilingly.

— King Lear

I drink to the general joy of the whole table.

— Macbeth

I wish you all the Joy that you can wish.

— The Merchant of Venice

O God! that men should put an enemy
in their mouths to steal away their
brains: that we should, with joy,
pleasance, revel, and applause, transform
ourselves into beasts.

— Othello

Women are angels, wooing;
Things won are done; joy's soul lies in the doing:
That she belov'd knows nought that knows not this:
Men prize the thing ungain'd more than it is.

— Troilus and Cressida

JUDGMENT

An upright judge, a learned Judge!

— *Merchant of Venice*

And then the justice
In fair round belly with good capon lined.

— *As You Like It*

O Judgment! thou art fled to brutish beasts,
And men have lost their reasons!

— *Julius Caesar*

His years but young, but his experience old;
His head unmellowed, but his judgment ripe.

— *Two Gentleman of Verona*

Gently to hear, kindly to judge.

— *King Henry V*

Thiefs for their robbery have authority, when
judges steal themselves.

— *Merchant of Venice*

My salad days,
When I was green in Judgment.

— *Antony and Cleopatra*

You cannot call it love, for at your age
The hey-day in the blood is tame, it's humble,
And waits upon the judgment.

— *Hamlet*

A Daniel come to judgment! yea, a Daniel!
O wise young judge, how I do honour thee!

— *The Merchant of Venice*

Why, all the souls that were forfeit once;
And He that might the vantage best have took,
Found out the remedy. How would you be,
If He, which is the top of judgment, should
But judge you as you are?

— *Measure for Measure*

What judgment shall I dread, doing no wrong?

— *The Merchant of Venice*

Beauty is bought by judgment of the eye,
Not utter'd by base sale of chapmen's tongues.

— *Love's Labour's Lost*

The fire seven times tried this:
Seven times tried that judgment is
That did never choose amiss.
Some there be that shadows kiss;
Such have but a shadow's bliss.

— *The Merchant of Venice*

A man that fortune's buffets and rewards,
Hast ta'en with equal thanks: and bless'd are those
Whose blood and judgment are so well co-mingled
That they are not a pipe for fortune's finger
To sound what stop she please.

— *Hamlet*

JUSTICE

Thrice is he arm'd that hath his quarrel just,
And he but naked, though lock'd up in steel,
Whose conscience with injustice is corrupted.

— *Henry VI*

Thyself shalt see the act;
For, as thou urgest justice, be assur'd
Thou shalt have justice, more than thou desir'st.

— *The Merchant of Venice*

And liberty plucks justice by the nose.

— *Measure for Measure*

This even-handed Justice.

— *Macbeth*

Let the great gods,
That keep this dreadful pother o'er our heads,
Find out their enemies now. Tremble, thou wretch,
That hast within thee undivulged crimes,
Unwhipp'd of Justice.

— *King Lear*

The justice of it pleases.

— *Othello*

A man may see how this world goes with
no eyes. Look with thine ears; See how
yond justice rails upon yond simple
thief. Hark, in thine ear; change
places; and, handy-dandy, which is the
justice, which is the thief?

— *King Lear*

KINDNESS

Yet do I fear thy nature;
It is too full o'the milk of human kindness
To catch the nearest way.

— Macbeth

She shall watch all night;
And if she chance to nod I'll rail and brawl,
And with the clamour keep her still awake.
This is the way to kill a wife with kindness.

— The Taming of the Shrew

Is she kind as she is fair?
For beauty lives with kindness.
Love doth to her eyes repair,
To help him of his blindness;
And, being help'd, inhabits there.

— Two Gentlemen of Verona

I must be cruel, only to be kind.

— Hamlet

For herein fortune shows herself more kind
Than is her custom: it is still her use,
To let the wretched man outlive his wealth,
To view with hollow eye and wrinkled brow,
An age of poverty.

— The Merchant of Venice

A little more than kin, and less than kind.

— Hamlet

KING

A king of shreds and patches.

— Hamlet

Ay, every inch a king.

— King Lear

There's such a divinity doth hedge a king,
That treason can but peep to what it would.

— Hamlet

Not all the water in the rough rude sea
Can wash the balm from an anointed king.

— Richard II

Uneasy lies the head that wears a crown.

— Henry IV

Nice customs curtesy to great kings.

— Henry V

For God's sake, let us sit upon the ground
And tell sad stories of the death of kings.

— Richard II

And what have kings that privates have not too,
Save ceremony, save general ceremony.

— Henry V

Now is the winter of our discontent
Made glorious summer by this sun of york.

— Richard III

A bloody deed; almost as bad, good mother,
As kill a king, and marry with his brother.

— Hamlet

A man may fish with the worm that hath
eat of a king, and eat of the fish that
hath fed of that worm.

— *Hamlet*

Now the king drinks to Hamlet!

— *Hamlet*

If chance will have me king, why, chance
may crown me.

— *Macbeth*

God save the king! will no man say, amen?
Am I both priest and clerk? well then, amen.

— *Richard II*

Is the chair empty? is the sword unsway'd?
Is the king dead? the empire unpossess'd?

— *Richard III*

A mockery king of snow.

— *Richard II*

You may my glories and my State depose,
But not my griefs: still am I king of those.

— *Richard II*

So doth the greater glory dim the less.
A substitute shines brightly as a king
Until a king be by, and then his State
Empties itself, as doth an inland brook
Into the main of waters.

— *The Merchant of Venice*

Here will be an old abusing of God's patience,
and the king's English.

— *The Merry Wives of Windsor*

No ceremony that to great ones 'longs,
Not the king's crown, nor the deputed sword,
The marshal's truncheon, nor the judge's robe,
Become them with one half so good a grace
As mercy does.

-- *Measure for Measure*

If I were as tedious as a king, I could
find in my heart to bestow it all of
your worship.

— Much Ado About Nothing.

O God! I could be bounded in a nutshell,
and count myself a king of infinite space,
were it not that I have bad dreams.

— Hamlet

Such thanks
As fits a king's remembrance.

— Hamlet

Had I but serv'd my God with half the zeal
I serv'd my king, he would not in mine age
Have left me naked to mine enemies.

— Henry VIII

There was the weight that pull'd me down. cromwell!
The king has gone beyond me: all my glories
In that one woman I have lost for ever.

— Henry VIII

I have misus'd the king's press damnably.

— Henry IV

The skipping king, he ambled up and down
with shallow jesters and rash bavin wits.

— Henry IV

Under which king, Bezonian? Speak, or die!

— Henry IV

Every Subject's duty is the king's; but
every Subject's soul is his own.

— Henry V

Heaven is above all yet; there sits a judge,
That no king can corrupt.

— Henry VIII

GLOUCESTER : Is't not the king?
LEAR : Ay, every inch a king.

— King Lear

KISSING

Take, O take those lips away,
That so sweetly were forsworn:
And those eyes, the break of day,
Lights that do mislead the morn;
But my kisses bring again, bring again;
Seals of love, but seal'd in vain, seal'd in vain.

— *Measure for Measure*

There is gold, and here
My bluest veins to kiss; a hand that kings,
Have lipp'd, and trembled kissing.

— *Antony and Cleopatra*

All you that kiss our lady peace at home.

— *Henry IV*

It is not a fashion for the maids in France
to kiss before they are married.

— *Henry V*

Speak, cousin, or, if you cannot, stop his
mouth with a kiss.

— *Much Ado About Nothing*

I kiss'd thee ere I kill'd thee.

— *Othello*

The fire seven times tried this;
Seven times tried that Judgment is
That did never choose amiss.
Some there be that shadows kiss;
Such have but a shadow's bliss.

— *The Merchant of Venice*

KNAVE

'Gainst knaves and thieves men shut their gate.

— *Twelfth Night*

A knave; a rascal: an eater of broken meats;
a base, proud, shallow, beggarly, thee-suited,
hundred pound, filthy, worsted-stocking knave...

— *King Lear*

A pestilent complete knave! and the woman
hath found him already.

— *Othello*

A slipper and subtle knave, a finder-out of
occasions.

— *Othello*

What trade, thou knave? thou naughty
knave, what trade?

— *Julius Caesar*

A rascally yea-forsooth knave.

— *Henry IV*

There's ne'er a villain dwelling in all Denmark,
But he's an arrant knave.

— *Hamlet*

My desolation does begin to make
A better life. 'Tis paltry to be Caesar;
Not being fortune, he's but fortune's knave,
A minister of her will; and it is great
To do that thing that ends all other deeds,
Which shackles accidents, and bolts up change,
Which sleeps, and never palates more the dug,
The beggar's nurse and Caesar's.

— *Antony and Cleopatra*

KNOW

O! that a man might know
The end of this day's business, ere it come;
But it sufficeth that the day will end,
And then the end is known.

— Julius Caesar

For I have neither wit, nor words, nor worth,
Action, nor utterance, nor power of speech,
To stir men's blood; I only speak right on;
I tell you that which you yourselves do know.

— Julius Caesar

I swear 'tis better to be much abus'd
Than but to know 't a little.

— Othello

He that is robb'd, not wanting what is stol'n,
Let him not know 't and he's not robb'd at all.

— Othello

Demand me nothing; what you know, you know;
From this time forth I never will speak word.

— Othello

Yet this shall I ne'er know, but live in doubt,
Till my bad angel fire my good one out.

— Sonnet-144

Dost know this water-fly?

— Hamlet

Constant you are,
But yet a woman; and for secrecy,

No lady closer; for I well believe
Thou wilt not utter what thou dost not know.

— *Henry IV*

All! I know not what ye call all.

— *Henry IV*

You would play upon me; you would
seem to know my stops; you would
pluck out the heart of my mystery;
you would sound me from my lowest note
to the top of my compass.

— *Hamlet*

I know thee not, old man: fall to thy prayers;
How ill white hairs become a fool and jester!
I have long dream'd of such a kind of man,
So surfeit-swell'd, so old, and so profane.

— *Henry IV*

LADY

Henceforth,
The white hand of a lady fever thee,
shake thou to look on 't.

— Antony and Cleopatra

The lady doth protest too much, methinks.

— Hamlet

Constant you are,
But yet a woman : and for secrecy,
No lady closer: for I well believe
Thou wilt not utter what thou dost not know.

— Henry IV

Lady the brach may stand by the fire and stink.

— King Lear

Some men must love my lady, and some Joan.

— Love's Labour's Lost

For, as I am a man, I think this lady
To be my child Cordelia.

— King Lear

He capers nimbly in a lady's chamber
To the lascivious pleasing of a lute

— Richard III

LAW

But in these nice sharp quillets of the law,
Good faith, I am no wiser than a daw.

— *Henry VI*

The first thing we do, let's kill all the lawyers.

— *Henry VI*

The bloody book of law
You shall yourself read in the bitter letter
After your own sense.

— *Othello*

Wrest once the law to your authority:
To do a great right, do a little wrong.

— *The Merchant of Venice*

We must not make a scarecrow of the law,
Setting it upto fear the birds of prey,
And let it keep one shape, till custom make it.
Their perch and not their terror.

— *Measure for Measure*

Still you keep o'the windy side of the law.

— *Twelfth Night*

The world is not thy friend, nor the world's law.

— *Romeo and Juliet*

Is the law of our side if I say ay?

— *Romeo and Juliet*

My deeds upon my head! I crave the law.

— *The Merchant of Venice*

The court awards it, and the law doth give it.

— *The Merchant of Venice*

LIE

The Retort courteous;.......the quip modest;
..........the Reply churlish;.........the Reproof
valiant;......the countercheck Quarrelsome;
.....the lie with circumstance;........
the lie Direct.

— *As You Like It*

O! the world hath not a sweeter creature;
She might lie by an emperor's side and
command him tasks.

— *Othello*

For my part, if a lie may do thee grace,
I'll gild it with the happiest terms I have.

— *Henry IV*

That's a fair thought to lie between maids' legs.

— *Hamlet*

To lapse in fulness
Is sorer than to lie for need, and falsehood
Is worse in kings than beggars.

— *Cymbeline*

Under the green wood tree
Who loves to lie with me,
And turn his merry note
Unto the sweet bird's throat,
Come hither, come hither, come hither:

— *As You Like It*

Between the acres of the rye,
With a hey, and a ho, and a hey nonino,
These pretty country folks would lie,
In the spring time.

— *As You Like It*

LIFE

We are such stuff
As dreams are made on and our little life
Is rounded with a sleep

— *The Tempest*

Life's but a walking shadow, a poor player,
That struts and frets his hour upon the stage
And then is heard no more; it is a tale
Told by an idiot, full of sound and fury,
Signifying nothing.

— *Macbeth*

Uncertain life and sure death.

— *All's Well That Ends Well*

All the world's a stage,
And all the men and women merely players.

— *As You Like It*

Life is as tedious as a twice-told tale
Vexing the dull ear of a drowsy man.

— *King John*

When we are born, we cry that we are come
To this great stage of fools.

— *King Lear*

Unkindness may do much;
And his unkindness may defeat my life,
But never taint my love.

— *Othello*

Slave! I have set my life upon a cast,
And I will stand the hazard of the die.
I think there be six Richmonds in the field.

— *Richard III*

And let me the canakin clink:
A soldier's a man;
A life's but a span;
Why then let a soldier drink.

— *Othello*

Think'st thou I'd make a life of jealousy,
To follow still the changes of the moon
With fresh suspicious? No; to be once in doubt
Is once to be resolved.

— *Othello*

My life upon her faith!

— *Othello*

Thou art a fellow of a good respect;
Thy life hath had some smatch of honour in it.

— *Julius Caesar*

He, only, in a general honest thought
And common good to all, made one of them.
His life was gentle, and the elements
So mix'd in him that Nature might stand up,
And say to all the world, 'This was a man!'

— *Julius Caesar*

Thriftless ambition, that wilt ravin up
Thine own life's means!

— *Macbeth*

Nothing in his life
Became him like the leaving it; he died
As one that had been studied in his death
To throw away the dearest thing he owed
As 't were a careless trifle.

— *Macbeth*

Thou art a fellow of a good respect;
Thy life hath had some smatch of honour in it.

— *Julius Caesar*

This day I breathed first; time is come round,
And where I did begin, there shall I end;
My life is run his compass.

— *Julius Caesar*

O excellent! I love long life better than figs.

— *Antony and Cleopatra*

I do not set my life at a pin's fee;
And for my soul, what can it do to that,
Being a thing immortal as itself?

— *Hamlet*

I bear a charmed life.

— *Macbeth*

You take my house when you do take the prop,
That doth sustain my house; you take my life
When you do take the means whereby I live.

— *The Merchant of Venice*

I fetch my life and being
From men of royal siege.

— *Othello*

The idea of her life shall sweetly creep
Into his study of imagination,
And every lovely organ of her life
Shall come apparell'd in more precious habit,
More moving — delicate, and full of life
Into the eye and prospect of his soul.

— *Much Ado About Nothing*

Like madness is the glory of this life.

— *Timon of Athens*

For the life to come, I sleep out the thought of it.

— *The Winter's Tale*

Life's uncertain voyage.

— *Timon of Athens*

Be absolute for death; either death or life
Shall thereby be the sweeter.

— *Measure for Measure*

'Tis one thing to be tempted, Escalus,
Another thing to fall. I not deny,
The Jury, passing on the prisoner's life,
May in the sworn twelve have a thief or two
Guiltier than him they try.

— *Measure for Measure*

Confusion now hath made his masterpiece!
Most sacrilegious murder hath broke ope
The Lord's anointed temple, and stole thence
The life o'the building!

— *Macbeth*

And my poor fool is hang'd! No, no, no life!
Why should a dog, a horse, a rat, have life,
And thou no breath at all? Thou't come no more,
Never, never, never, never, never!
Pray you, undo this button.

— *King Lear*

The weariest and most loathed worldly life
That age, ache, penury, and imprisonment
Can lay on nature, is a paradise
To what we fear of death.

— *Measure for Measure*

LIGHT

But, soft! what light through yonder window breaks?
It is the east, and Juliet is the sun.

— Remeo and Juliet

O! so light a foot
Will ne'er wear out the everlasting flint.

— Romeo and Juliet

For a light wife doth make a heavy husband.

— The Merchant of Venice

Truth will come to light; murder cannot be hid long.

— The Merchant of Venice

Had she been light, like you,
Of such a merry, nimble, stirring spirit,
She might ha' been a grandam ere she died;
And so may you; for a light heart lives long.

— Love's Labour's Lost

This battle fares like to the morning's war,
When dying clouds contend with growing light,
What time the shepherd, blowing of his nails,
Can neither call it perfect day nor light.

— Henry VI

Seneca cannot be too heavy, nor Plautus too light.

— Hamlet

LIPS

And steal immortal blessing from her lips,
Who, even in pure and vestal modesty,
Still blush, as thinking their own kisses sin.

— Romeo and Juliet

Eternity was in our lips and eyes,
Bliss in our brows bent.

— Antony and Cleopatra

His coward lips did from their colour fly,
And that same eye whose bend doth awe the world,
Did lose his lustre.

— Julius Caesar

Beauty's ensign yet
Is crimson in thy lips and in thy cheeks,
And death's pale flag is not advanced there.

— Romeo and Juliet

Item, two lips, indifferent red; Item,
Two grey eyes with lids to them;
Item, one neck, one chin, and so forth.

— Twelfth Night

My mistress' eyes are nothing like the sun;
Coral is far more red than her lips' red;
If snow be white, why then her breasts are dun;
If hairs be wires, black wires grow on her head.

— Sonnet-130

Your Caesar's father oft,
When he hath mus'd of taking kingdoms in,
Bestow'd his lips on that unworthy place,
As it rain'd kisses.

— Antony and Cleopatra

LOOK

Unless I look on Silvia in the day,
There is no day for me to look upon.

— *Two Gentlemen of Verona.*

I am proverb'd with a grandsire phrase;
I'll be a candle-holder, and look on.

— *Romeo and Juliet*

Her wanton spirits look out
At every joint and motive of her body.

— *Troilus and Cressida*

If you can look into the seeds of time,
And say which grain will grow and which will not.

— *Macbeth*

Look like the innocent flower,
But be the serpent under't.

— *Macbeth*

Set honour in one eye and death i' the other,
And I will look on both indifferently.

— *Julius Caesar*

Look here, upon this picture, and on this.

— *Hamlet*

Henceforth,
The white hand of a lady fever thee,
Shake thou to look on't.

— *Antony and Cleopatra*

LOVE

When my love swears that she is made of truth,
I do believe her, though I know she lies.

— *Sonnets*-138

But love is blind, and lovers cannot see
The pretty follies that themselves commit.

— *Merchant of Venice*

Men have died from time to time and worms
have eaten them, but not for love.

— *As You Like It*

Doubt thou the stars are fire;
Doubt that the sun doth move;
Doubt truth to be a liar;
But never doubt I love.

— *Hamlet*

Sigh no more, ladies, sigh no more,
Men were deceivers ever,
One foot in sea and one on shore,
To one thing constant never.

— *Much Ado About Nothing*

Love is a smoke raised with the fume of sighs;
Being purged, a fire sparkling in lovers' eyes;
Being vex'd, a sea nourished with lovers' tears:
What is it else? a madness most discreet,
A chocking gall and persevering sweet.

— *Romeo and Juliet*

And then the lover,
Sighing like furnace, with a woeful ballad
Made to his mistress' eyebrow.

— *As You Like It*

Affection is a coal that must be cooled;
Else, suffered, it will set the heart on fire.

— Venus and Adonis

For aught that I could ever read
could ever hear by tale or history,
The course of true love never bid seem smooth.

— A Midsummer Night's Dream

Speak low, if you speak love.

— Much Ado About Nothing

My bounty is as the boundless sea,
My love as deep, the more I give to thee
The more I have, for both are infinite.

— Romeo and Juliet

Love sought is good, but given unsought is better.

— Twelfth Night

She's beautiful and therefore to be woo'd:
She's a woman, therefore to be won.

— Henry VI

Love is a familiar. Love is a devil.
There is no evil angel but love.

— Love's Labour's Lost

Speak of me as I am......one that
loved not wisely but too well.

— Othello

They do not love that do not show their love.

— The Two Gentlemen of Verona

Love comforteth like sunshine after rain.

— Venus and Adonis

Let me not to the marriage of true minds
Admit impediments. Love is not love
which alters when it alteration finds,
or bends with the remover to remove,
Oh no! It is an ever-fixed mark
That looks on tempests and is never shaken.

It is the star to every wandering bark,
Whose worth's unknown, although his height be taken.

— *Sonnet-116*

What is mine is yours, and what is yours is mine.

— *Measure for Measure*

But, soft! what light through yonder window breaks?
It is the east, and Juliet is the sun.

— *Romeo and Juliet*

Kiss me, Kate!

— *The Taming of the Shrew*

See how she leans her cheek upon her hand!
Oh, that I were a glove upon that land,
That I might touch that cheek!

— *Romeo and Juliet*

Shall I compare thee to a summer's day?
Thou art more lovely and more temperate.

— *Sonnet-18*

O Romeo, Romeo, wherefore art thou Romeo?
Deny thy father and refuse thy name,
Or, if thou wilt not, be but sworn my love
And I'll no longer be a capulet.

— *Romeo and Juliet*

Goodnight! Goodnight!
Parting is such sweet sorrow
That I shall say goodnight till it be morrow.

— *Romeo and Juliet*

When he shall die,
Take him and cut him out in little stars,
And he will make the face of heaven so fine
That all the world will be in love with night.

— *Romeo and Juliet*

But we are soldiers;
And may that soldier a mere recreant prove,
That means not, hath not, or is not in love.

— *Troilus and Cressida*

But since he died, and poets better prove,
Theirs for their style I'll read, his for his love.

— *Sonnet-32*

Excellent wretch! perdition catch my soul
But I do love thee! and when I love thee not,
Chaos is come again.

— *Othello*

MADNESS

Though this be madness, yet there is method in't.

— *Hamlet*

Have we eaten on the insane root
That takes the reason prisoner?

— *Macbeth*

That he is mad, 'tis true; 'tis true 'tis pity:
And pity 'tis 'tis true.

— *Hamlet*

Out, damned spot! out, I say! one, two, why,
then 'tis time to do it. Hell is murky!

— *Macbeth*

Madness in great ones must not unwatched go.

— *Hamlet*

Is this a dagger which I see before me,
The handle toward my hand? come let me clutch thee.

— *Macbeth*

Art thou but
A dagger of the mind, a false creation
proceeding from the heat-oppressed brain?

— *Macbeth*

It is an accustomed action with her to
seem thus washing her hands. I have
known her continue in this a quarter
of an hour.

— *Macbeth*

MAN

But man, proud man,
Drest in a little brief anthority,
Most ignorant of what he's most assur'd,
His glassy essence, like an angry ape,
Plays such fantastic tricks before high heaven,
As make the angels weep.

— *Measure for Measure*

His life was gentle, and the elements,
So mix'd in him that Nature might stand up,
And say to all the world "This was a man!"

— *Julius Caesar*

We are such stuff
As dreams are made on, and our little life
Is rounded with a sleep.

— *The Tempest*

How beauteous mankind is! o brave new world,
That has such people in it.

— *The Tempest*

I have more flesh than another man, and
therefore more frailty.

— *Henry IV*

O! that this too too solid flesh would melt,
Thaw and resolve itself into a dew.

— *Hamlet*

Kindness in women, not their beauteous looks,
Shall win my love.

— *The Taming of the Shrew*

Sigh no more, ladies, sigh no more.
men were deceivers ever;
one foot in sea, and one on shore,
To one thing constant never.

— *Much Ado About Nothing*

What a piece of work is a man! How noble in reason! How infinite in faculty! In form, in moving, how express and admirable! In action how like an angel! In apprehension how like a God! The beauty of the world! The paragon of animals!

— *Hamlet*

God made him, and therefore let him pass for a man.

— *The Merchant of Venice*

'Ban, 'Ban, Ca-caliban,
Has a new master-Get a new man.

— *The Tempest*

An honest exceeding poor man.

— *The Merchant of Venice*

I think the king is but a man, as I am:
the violet smells to him as it doth to me.

— *Henry V*

I have a man's mind, but a woman's might.
How hard it is for women to keep counsel!

— *Julius Caesar*

MARRIAGE

The ancient saying is no heresy,
Hanging and wiving go by destiny.

— Merchant of Venice

A young man married is a man that's marr'd.

— All's Well That Ends Well

A light wife doth make a heavy husband.

— Merchant of Venice

Crabbed age and youth cannot live together:
Youth is full of pleasance, age is full of care.

— Passionate Pilgrim

That it went hand in hand even with the vow,
I made to her in marriage.

— Hamlet

It seems the marriage with his brother's wife,
Has crept too near his conscience.

— Henry VIII

O curse of marriage!
That we can call these delicate creatures ours,
And not their appetites. I had rather be a toad,
And live upon the vapour of a dungeon,
Than keep a corner in the thing I love
For other's uses.

— Othello

Let me not to the marriage of true minds,
Admit impediments.

— Sonnet-116

MEETING

Journeys end in lovers meeting.
Every wise man's son doth know.

—Twelfth Night

FIRST WITCH :	When shall we three meet again, In thunder, lightning or in rain?
SECOND WITCH :	When the hurly burly's done, When the batte's lost and won.

— Macbeth

You have displaced the mirth, broke the good meeting,
With most admir'd disorder.

— Macbeth

Our stern alarums changed to merry meetings;
Our dreadful marches to delightful measures.

— Richard III

Trip no further, pretty sweeting;
Journeys end in lovers meeting,
Every wise man's son doth know.

— Twelfth Night

If we do meet again, why, we shall smile!
If not, why then, this parting was well made.

— Julius Caesar

O most pernicious woman!
O villain, villain, smiling, damned villain!
My tables, — meet it is I set it down,
That one may smile, and smile, and be a villain:
At least I'm sure it may be so in Denmark.

— Hamlet

MEMORY

When to the sessions of sweet silent thought,
I summon up remembrance of things past,
I sigh the lack of many a thing I sought,
And with old woes new wail my dear time's waste.

— *Sonnets*-30

What's past is prologue.

— *The Tempest*

Die two months ago, and not forgotten yet?
Then there's hope a great man's memory
may outlive his life half a year; but,
by'r lady, he must build churches then

— *Hamlet*

These are begot in the ventricle of
memory, nourished in the womb of
pia mater, and delivered upon the
mellowing of occasion.

— *Love's Labour's Lost*

That memory, the warder of the brain,
Shall be a fume.

— *Macbeth*

O! it comes o'er my memory,
As doth the raven o'er the infected house,
Boding to all.

— *Othello*

The memory be green.

— *Hamlet*

Yea, from the table of my memory
I'll wipe away all trivial fond records,
All saws of books, all forms, all pressures past,
That youth and observation copied there.

— *Hamlet*

MERCY

The quality of mercy is not strain'd;
It droppeth as the gentle rain from heaven
Upon the place beneath: it is twice blest;
It blesseth him that gives and him that takes:
'Tis mightiest in the mightiest: it becomes
The throned monarch better than his crown:
....
And earthly power doth then show likest God's
when mercy seasons Justice.

— *Merchant of Venice*

Sweet mercy is nobility's true badge.

— *Titus Andronicus*

No beast so fierce but knows some touch of pity.

— *Richard III*

The quality of mercy is not strained,
It droppeth as the gentle rain from heaven.

— *Merchant of Venice*

Whereto serves mercy
But to confront the visage of offence?

— *Hamlet*

Nothing emboldens sin so much as mercy.

— *Timon of Athens*

Fare thee well; and God have mercy upon
one of our Souls! He may have mercy
upon mine, but my hope in better: and
so look to thyself.

— *Twelfth Night*

He is gone, he is gone
And we cast away moan :
God ha' mercy on his soul !

— *Hamlet*

MIDNIGHT

'Tis now the very witching time of night,
When churchyards yawn and hell itself breathes
but contagion to this world.

— *Hamlet*

What doth gravity out of his bed at midnight?

— *Henry IV*

We have heard the chimes at midnight.

— *Henry IV*

How now, you secret, black, and midnight hags!

— *Macbeth*

Look, here's the warrant, claudio, for thy death:
'Tis now dead midnight, and by eight to-morrow.
Thou must be made immortal.

— *Measure for Measure*

The iron tongue of midnight hath told twelve;
Lovers, to bed: 'tis almost fairy time.

— *A Midsummer Night's Dream*

Not to be a-bed after midnight is to be up betimes.
....To be up after midnight and to go
to bed then, is early; so that to go to
bed after midnight is to go to bed betimes.

— *Twelfth Night*

MIND

Canst thou minister to a mind diseased,
Pluck from the memory a rooted sorrow,
Raze out the written troubles of the brain,
And with some sweet oblivious antidote
cleanse the stuff'd bosom of that perilous matter
which weighs upon the heart?

— *Macbeth*

O what a noble mind is here o'er thrown!

....

......that noble and most sovereign reason,
Like sweet bells jangled, out of tune and harsh.

— *Hamlet*

Thy wish was father, Harry, to that thought.

— *Henry IV*

There is nothing either good or bad but
thinking makes it so.

— *Hamlet*

In my mind's eye, Horatio.

— *Hamlet*

When the mind's free,
The body's delicate.

— *King Lear*

Men that hazard all
Do it in hope of fair advantages;
A golden mind stoops not to shows of dross.

— *The Merchant of Venice*

I like not fair terms and a villain's mind.

— *The Merchant of Venice*

Now, the melancholy god protect thee, and the tailor make thy doublet of changeable taffeta, for thy mind is a very opal.

— *Twelfth Night*

MISERY

Misery acquaints a man with strange bed-fellows.

— *The Tempest*

O! what a rogue and peasant slave am I.

— *Hamlet*

Tomorrow, and tomorrow, and tomorrow,
Creeps in this petty pace from day to day,
To the last syllable of recorded time.

— *Macbeth*

We have seen better days

— *Timon of Athens*

There's small choice in rotten apples.

— *The Taming of the Shrew*

The worst is not
So long as we can say, "This is the worst".

— *King Lear*

When sorrows come, they come not single spies,
But in battalions.

— *Hamlet*

One woe doth tread upon another's heel,
So fast they follow.

— *Hamlet*

Sweet are the uses of adversity.

— *As You Like It*

MISFORTUNE

When sorrows come, they come not single spies,
But in battalions.

— Hamlet

I am a man
More sinned against than sinning.

— King Lear

Men shut their doors against a setting sun.

— Timon of Athens

One writ with me in sour misfortune's book.

— Romeo and Juliet

This is that very mab
That plats the manes of horses in the night;
And bakes the elf-locks in foul sluttish hairs,
which once untangled much misfortune bodes;
This is the hag, when maids lie on their backs,
That presses them and learns them first to bear,
Making them women of good carriage.

— .Romeo and Juliet

If it be my luck, so; if not, happy man be his dole.

— The Merry Wives of Windsor

MONEY

Who steals my purse steals trash.

— *Othello*

O, what a world of vile ill-favoured faults,
Looks handsome in three hundred pounds a-year.

— *The Merry Wives of Windsor*

If money goes before, all ways do lie upon.

— *The Merry Wives of Windsor*

Neither a borrower nor a lender be.

— *Hamlet*

He is well paid that is well satisfied.

— *The Merchant of Venice*

He that wants money, means, and content is
without three good friends.

— *As You Like It*

'Fair Sir, you spat on me on wednesday last;
You spurn'd me such a day; another time
You call'd me dog; and for these courtesies
I'll lend you thus much moneys?'

— *The Merchant of Venice*

Put money in thy purse.

— *Othello*

Nothing comes amiss, so money comes withal.

— *The Taming of the Shrew*

MOON

O, swear not by the moon, the inconstant moon,
That monthly changes in her circled orb,
Lest that thy love prove likewise variable.

— *Romeo and Juliet*

'Tis like the howling of Irish wolves
against the moon.

— *As You Like It*

Let us be Diana's foresters, gentlemen of
the shade, minions of the moon.

— *Henry IV*

Slips of yew
Sliver'd in the moon's eclipse.

— *Macbeth*

To live a barren sister all your life,
chanting faint hymns to the cold fruitless moon.

— *A Midsummer Night's Dream*

Think'st thou I'd make a life of Jealousy,
To follow still the changes of the moon
with fresh suspicions? No; to be once in doubt.
Is once to be resolved.

— *Othello*

The mortal moon hath her eclipse endur'd,
And the sad augurs mock their own presage.

— *Sonnet-107*

MORNING

Full many a glorious morning have I seen
Flatter the mountain-tops with sovereign eye.

— *Sonnets*-33

See how the morning opes her golden gates,
And takes her farewell of the glorious sun!

— *Henry VI*

Say that she rail; why then I'll tell her plain
She sings as sweetly as a nightingale:
Say that she frown; I'll say she looks as clear,
As morning roses newly wash'd with dew:

— *The Taming of the Shrew*

More matter for a May morning.

— *Twelfth Night*

'Tis almost morning, I would have thee gone;
And yet no further than a wanton's bird,
Who lets it hop a little from her hand,
Like a poor prisoner in his twisted gyves,
And with a silk thread plucks it back again,
So loving-jealous of his liberty.

— *Romeo and Juliet*

But, soft! methinks I scent the morning air.

— *Hamlet*

This battle fares like to the morning's war,
When dying clouds contend with growing light,
What time the shepherd, blowing of his nails,
Can neither call it perfect day nor night.

— *Henry VI*

MORTALITY

........Who would fardels bear,
To grunt and sweat under a weary life,
But that the dread of something after death,
The undiscover'd country from whose bourn
No traveller returns, puzzles the will
And makes us rather bear those ills we have
Than fly to others that we know not of?

— *Hamlet*

All that live must die,
Passing through nature to eternity.

— *Hamlet*

A man can die but once. We owe God a death.

— *Henry IV*

Men must endure
Their going hence even as their coming hither.

— *King Lear*

How oft when men are at the point of death
Have they been merry!

— *Romeo and Juliet*

Life's but a walking shadow, a poor player,
That struts and frets his hour upon the stage
And then is heard no more. It is a tale
Told by an idiot, full of sound and fury,
Signifying nothing.

— *Macbeth*

All the world's a stage,
And all the men and women merely players.

— *As You Like It*

MOTHER

I am yet so near the manners of
my mother; that upon the least occasion
more mine eyes will tell tales of me.

— *Twelfth Night*

Thou art thy mother's glass, and she in thee,
calls back the lovely April of her prime.

— *Sonnet-3*

Alas! poor country;
Almost afraid to know itself. It cannot
Be call'd our mother, but our grave.

— *Macbeth*

And all my mother came into mine eyes
And gave me up to tears.

— *Henry V*

O wonderful son, that can so astonish a mother!

— *Hamlet*

Some Jay of Italy,
Whose mother was her paiting, hath betray'd him:
Poor I am stale, a garment out of fashion.

— *Cymbeline*

Thou hast never in thy life,
Show'd thy dear mother any courtesy:

— *Coriolanus*

MURDER

The great king of kings
Hath in the tables of his law commanded
That thou shalt do no murder.

— *Richard III*

Cut off even in the blossoms of my sin,
Unhousel'd, disappointed, unaneled,
No reckoning made, but sent to my account
with all my imperfections on my head.

— *Hamlet*

Murder most foul, as in the best it is
But this most foul, strange, and unnatural.

— *Hamlet*

Yet who would have thought the old man to
have had so much blood in him?

— *Macbeth*

Revenge his foul and most unnatural murder.

— *Hamlet*

Truth will come to light; murder cannot be hid long.

— *The Merchant of Venice*

Though in the trade of war I have slain men,
Yet do I hold it very stuff o' the conscience
To do no contriv'd murder: I lack iniquity
Sometimes to do me service.

— *Othello*

No place, indeed, should murder sanctuarize.

— *Hamlet*

MUSIC

Orphens with his lute made trees,
And the mountain tops that freeze,
Bow themselves when he did sing:
To his music plants and flowers
Ever sprung: as sun and showers,
There had made a lasting spring.

— *Henry VIII*

If music be the food of love, play on:
Give me excess of it, that, surfeiting,
The appetite may sicken, and so die.

— *Twelfth Night*

The man that hath no music in himself,
Nor is not moved with concord of sweet sounds,
Is fit for treasons, stratagems and spoils.

— *Merchant of Venice*

I am never merry when I hear sweet music.

— *The Merchant of Venice*

It will discourse most eloquent music.

— *Hamlet*

I have a reasonable good ear in music:
Let us have the tongs and the bones.

— *A Midsummer Night's Dream*

He makes a swan-like end
Fading in music.

— *The Merchant of Venice*

I will play the swan,
And die in music

— *Othello*

How sour sweet music is,
when time is broke, and no proportion kept!
So is it in the music of men's lives.

— Richard II

It is my soul that calls upon my name;
How silver-sweet sound lovers' tongues by night,
Like softest music to attending ears!

— Romeo and Juliet

This music crept by me upon the waters,
Allaying both their fury, and my passion,
with its sweet air.

— The Tempest

Music to hear, why hear'st thou music sadly?
Sweets with sweets war not, Joy delights in joy;
Why lov'st thou that which thou receiv'st not gladly,
Or else receiv'st with pleasure thine annoy?

— Sonnet-8

Music, moody food
of us that trade in love.

— Antony and Cleopatra

Though music oft hath such a charm
To make bad good, and good provoke to harm.

— Measure for Measure

Since once I sat upon a promontory,
And heard a mermaid on a dolphin's back
Uttering such dulcet and harmonious breath,
That the rude sea grew civil at her song,
And certain stars shot madly from their spheres,
To hear the sea-maid's music.

— A Midsummer Night's Dream

NATURE

One touch of nature makes the whole world kin.

— *Troilus and Cressida*

Nature teaches beasts to know their friends.

— *Coriolanus*

There's rose mary, that's for remembrance-pray you love, remember. And there is pansies, that's for thoughts.

— *Hamlet*

For you there's rosemary and rue, these keep,
Seeming and savor all the winter long.

— *The Winter's Tale*

The summer's flower is to the summer sweet,
Though to itself it only live and die.

— *Sonnet-94*

Why, this is very midsummer madness.

— *Twelfth Night*

A sad tale's best for winter.

— *The Winter's Tale*

Rough winds do shake the darling buds of May,
And summer's lease hath all too short a date.

— *Sonnet-18*

'Tis now the very witching time of night
When churchyards yawn and hell itself breathes out,
Contagion to this world.

— *Hamlet*

NIGHT

Come, civil night,
Thou sober-suited matron, all in black......
With thy black mantle.

— *Romeo and Juliet*

Come seeling night,
Scarf up the tender eye of pitiful day
...Light thickens; and the crow
Makes wing to the rooky wood.

— *Macbeth*

Light thickness: and the crow
Makes wings to the rooky wood.

— *Macbeth*

A sad tale's best for winter.

— *The Winter's Tale*

Rough winds do shake the darling buds of May,
And summer's lease hath all too short a date.

— *Sonnet-18*

'Tis now the very witching time of night,
When churchyards yawn and hell itself breaths out,
Contagion to this world.

— *Hamlet*

Why, this is very midsummer madness.

— *Twelfth Night*

The summer's flower is to the summer sweet,
Though to itself it only live and die.

— *Sonnet-94*

NOTHING

Nothing will come of nothing...
Nothing can be made out of nothing.

— King Lear

They are as sick that surfeit with too much, as they that starve with nothing.

— The Merchant of Venice

Do not put me to 't,
For I am nothing if not critical.

— Othello

Nothing comes amiss, so money comes withal.

— The Taming of the Shrew

My long sickness
Of health and living now begins to mend,
And nothing brings me all things.

— Timon of Athens

As who should say ' I am Sir oracle,
And when I ope my lips let no dog bark!'
O, my Antonio, I do know of these,
That therefore only are reputed wise,
For saying nothing.

— The Merchant of Venice

His promises were, as he then was, mighty;
But his performance, as he is now, nothing.

— Henry VIII

O! wither'd is the garland of the war,
The soldier's pole is fall'n; young boys and girls,

Are level now with men; the odds is gone,
And there is nothing left remarkable
Beneath the visiting moon.

— *Antony and Cleopatra*

OCCULT

Double, double toil and trouble,
Fire burn and cauldron bubble.

— *Macbeth*

CLENDOWER : I can call spirits from the vasty deep,
HOTSPUR : Why so can I, or so can any man;
But will they come when you do call for them?

— *Henry IV*

I'll break my staff,
Bury it certain fathoms in the earth,
And deeper than did ever plummer sound
I'll drown my book.

— *The Tempest*

Eye of newt and toe of frog,
Wool of bat and tongue of dog,
Adder's fork and blindworm's sting,
Lizard's leg and owlet's wing.
For a charm of powerful trouble,
Like a hell broth boil and bubble.

— *Macbeth*

He will discredit our mystery.

— *Measure for Measure*

OFFENCE

O, my offence is rank, it smells to heaven.

— Hamlet

I am not coveteous for gold,
But if it be a sin to covet honour
I am the most offending soul alive.

— King Henry V

Who is here so base that would be a bond man? If any, speak; for him have I offended, who is here so rude that would not be a Roman? If any, speak; for him have I offended. who is here so vile that will not love his country? if any, speak; for him have I offended. I pause for a reply.

— Julius Caesar

You are pictures out of doors,
Bells in your parlours, wild cats in your kitchens,
Saints in your injuries, devils being offended,
Players in your housewifery, and housewives in your beds.

— Othello

Alas! 'tiş true I have gone here and there,
And made myself a motley to the view,
Gor'd mine own thoughts, sold cheap what is most dear,
Made old offences of affections new.

— Sonnet-109

OLD

What should we speak of
when we are old as you?

— *Cymbeline*

There is an old poor man.

— *As You Like It*

Though I look old, yet I am strong and lusty;
For in my youth I never did apply
Hot and rebellious liquors in my blood.

— *As You Like It*

There live not three good men unchanged
in England, and one of them is fat
and grows old.

— *Henry IV*

There is a devil haunts thee in the
likeness of a fat old man; a turn of
man is thy companion.

— *Henry IV*

An old man, broken with the storms of state
Is come to lay his weary bones among ye;
Give him a little earth for charity.

— *Henry VIII*

You see me here, you gods, a poor old man,
As full of grief as age; wretched in both!

— *King Lear*

O, Sir! you are old;
Nature in you stands on the very verge
of her confine.

— *King Lear*

Young in limbs, in judgment old.

— *The Merchant of Venice*

I am too old to fawn upon a nurse,
Too far in years to be a pupil now.

— *Richard II*

And 'tis not hard, I think,
For men so old as we to keep the peace.

— *Romeo and Juliet*

Mark it, Cesario; it is old and plain.

— *Twelfth Night*

I am a very foolish, fond old man,
Fourscore and upward, not an hour more or less;

— *King Lear*

Lord, Lord, how subject we old men
are to this vice of lying!

— *Henry IV*

OPINION

Opinion's but a fool, that makes us scan
The outward habit by the inward man.

— Pericles

But in the gross and scope of my opinion,
This bodes some strange eruption to our state.

— Hamlet

What's the matter, you dissentious rogues,
That, rubbing the poor itch of your opinion,
Make yourselves scabs?

— Coriolanus

For he is superstitious grown of late,
Quite from the main opinion he held once
of fantasy, of dreams, and ceremonies.

— Julius Caesar

We will proceed no further in this business:
He hath honour'd me of late; and I have bought,
Golden opinions from all sorts of people.

— Macbeth

Why, now I see there's mettle in thee,
and even from this instant do build
on thee a better opinion than ever before.

— Othello

A plague of opinion! a man may wear
it on both sides, like a leather jerkin.

-- Troilus and Cressida

OPPORTUNITY

There is a tide in the affairs of men,
which taken at the flood, leads on to fortune.

— *Julius Caesar*

If chance will have me king, why
chance may crown me.

— *Macbeth*

This is the third time; I hope good
luck lies in odd numbers....There is
divinity in odd numbers, either in
nativity, chance or death.

— *The Merry Wives of Windsor*

Whose solid virtue
The shot of accident nor dart of chance,
Could neither graze nor pierce?

— *Othello*

Though I am not naturally honest, I
am so sometimes by chance.

— *The Winter's Tale*

And every fair from fair sometime declines,
By chance, or nature's changing course untrimm'd:

— *Sonnet-18*

Against ill chances men are ever merry,
But heaviness foreruns the good event.

— *Henry IV*

OWL

Then nightly sings the staring owl,
Tu-whit; tu-who, a merry note.

— *Love's Labour's Lost*

The owl, ...the fatal bellman,
which gives the stern'st good-night.

— *Macbeth*

It was the owl that shriek'd, the fatal bellman,
which gives the stern'st good-night.

— *Macbeth*

He wants the natural touch; for the poor wren,
The most diminutive of birds, will fight —
Her young ones in her nest-against the owl.

— *Macbeth*

Where the bee sucks, there suck I
In a cowslip's bell I lie,;
There I couch when owls do cry.

— *The Tempest*

The clamorous owl, that nightly hoots, and wanders,
At our quaint spirits.

— *A Midsummer Night's Dream*

A falcon, towering in her pride of place,
Was by a mousing owl hawk'd at and kill'd.

— *Macbeth*

PAIN

One fire burns out another's burning;
One pain is lessen'd by another's anguish.

— *Romeo and Juliet*

The labour we delight in physics pain.

— *Macbeth*

I would be loath to cast away my
speech, for besides that it is excellently
well penned, I have taken great pains
to con it.

— *Twelfth Night*

His present and your pains we thank you for;
When we have match'd our rackets to these balls,
We will in France, by God's grace, play a set
Shall strike his father's crown into the hazard.

— *Henry V*

Why, all delights are vain; but that most vain,
Which, with pain purchas'd, doth inherit pain,

— *Love's Labour's Lost*

And often did beguile her of her tears,
When I did speak of some distressful stroke
That my youth suffer'd. My story being done,
She gave me for my pains a world of sighs:

— *Othello*

PARTING

Good night, good night! parting is such sweet sorrow,
That I shall say good night till it be morrow.

— Romeo and Juliet

Think not, thou noble Roman,
That ever Brutus will go bound to Rome;
He bears too great a mind: but this same day
must end that work the ides of March begun;
And whether we shall meet again, I know not.
Therefore our everlasting farewell take:
For ever, and for ever, farewell, Cassius!
If we do meet again, why, we shall smile!
If not, why then, this parting was well made.

— Julius Caesar

The soul and body rive not more in parting,
Than greatness going off.

— Antony and Cleopatra

PASSION

Give me that man
That is not passion's slave, and I will wear him,
In my heart's core, ay, in my heart of heart.

— *Hamlet*

What to ourselves in passion we propose,
The passion ending, doth the purpose lose.

— *Hamlet*

Whom everything becomes, to chide, to laugh,
To weep: whose every passion fully strives
To make itself, in thee, fair and admir'd.

— *Antony and Cleopatra*

It is to be all made of fantasy,
All made of passion, and all made of wishes;
All adoration, duty, and observance;
All humbleness, all patience, and impatience;
All purity, all trial, all obeisance.

— *As You Like It*

His flaw'd heart,—
Alack! too weak the conflict to support;
'Twixt two extremes of passion, joy and grief,
Burst smilingly.

— *King Lear*

This music crept by me upon the waters,
Allaying both their fury, and my passion,
with its sweet air.

— *The Tempest*

PAST

The dark backward and abysm of time.

— The Tempest

What is past is prologue.

— The Tempest

What is done is done.

— Macbeth

Oh, call back yesterday, bid time return.

– Richard II

Confess yourself to heaven;
Repent what's past; avoid what is to come.

— Hamlet

O, thoughts of men accurst!
Past and to come seem best; things present, worst.

— Henry IV

To mourn a mischief that is past and gone
Is the next way to draw new mischief on.

— Othello

What's past, and what's to come, is strew'd with husks,
And formless ruin of oblivion.

— Troilus and Cressida

What's gone, and what's past help
Should be past grief.

— The Winter's Tale

I summon up remembrance of things past,
I sigh the lack of many a thing I sought,
And with old woes new wail my dear times' waste:

— Sonnet-30

PATIENCE

That which in mean men we intitle patience
Is pale cold cowardice in noble breasts.

— Richard II

Since you will buckle fortune on my back,
To bear her burthen, whether I will or no,
I must have patience to endure the load.

— Richard III

Here will be an old abusing of God's
patience, and the king's English.

— The Merry Wives of Windsor

And with a green and yellow melancholy,
She sat like patience on a monument,
Smiling at grief.

— Twelfth Night

I laugh'd him out of patience; and that night,
I laugh'd him into patience: and next morn,
Ere the ninth hour, I drunk him to his bed.

— Antony and Cleopatra

PATRIOTISM

Who is here so vile that will not love his country?
— *Julius Caesar*

One drop of blood drawn from thy country's bosom
Should grieve thee more than streams of foreign gore.
— *Henry VI*

PAY

There be many Caesars
Ere such another Julius, Britain is
A world by itself, and we will nothing pay
For wearing our own noses.

— *Cymbeline*

For every man that Bolinbroke hath press'd
To lift shrewd steel against our golden crown,
God for his Richard hath in heavenly pay
A glorious angel; then, if angels fight,
Weak men must fall, for heaven still guards the right.

— *Richard II*

Then can I grieve at grievances foregone,
And heavily from woe to woe tell o'er
The sad account of fore-bemoaned moan,
Which I new as if not paid before.

— *Sonnet-30*

PEACE

Peace, good pint pot!

— Henry IV

I speak of peace, while covert enmity,
Under the smile of safety wounds the world.

— Henry IV

All you that kiss our lady peace at home.

— Henry IV

In peace there's nothing so becomes a man
As modest stillness and humility.

— Henry V

A peace above all earthly dignities,
A still and quiet conscience.

— Henry VIII

In her days every man shall eat in safety
Under his own vine what he plants; and sing
The merry songs of peace to all his neighbours.

— Henry VIII

Why that the naked, poor, and mangled peace,
Dear nurse of arts, plenties and joyful births.

— Henry V

He gave his honours to the world again,
His blessed part to Heaven, and slept in peace.

— Henry VIII

The gods to-day stand friendly, that we may,
Lovers in peace, lead on our days to age!

— Julius Caesar

A moth of peace.

— *Othello*

Peace shall go sleep with Turks and infidels.

— *Richard II*

And 'tis not hard, I think,
For men so old as we to keep the peace.

— *Romeo and Juliet*

I am asham'd that women are so smile
To offer war where they should kneel for peace.

— *Taming of the Shrew*

Sleep dwell upon thine eyes, peace in thy breast!
Would I were sleep and peace, so sweet to rest!

— *Romeo and Juliet*

PEARL

One whose hand
Like the base Indian, threw a pearl away
Richer than all his tribe.

— *Othello*

Rich honesty dwells like a miser, Sir, in a poor house;
as your pearl in your foul oyster.

— *As You Like It*

I must go seek some dew-drops here,
And hang a pearl in every cowslip's ear.

— *A Midsummer Night's Dream*

Wedges of gold, great anchors, heaps of pearl,
Inestimable stones, unvalu'd Jewels,
All scatter'd in the bottom of the sea.

— *Richard III*

Then, must you speak
Of one that lov'd not wisely but too well;
Of one not easily jealous, but, being wrought,
Perplex'd in the extreme; of one whose hand,
Like the base Indian, threw a pearl away
Richer than all his tribe.

— *Othello*

PHILOSOPHY

For there was never yet philosopher
That could endure the toothache patiently.

— *Much Ado About Nothing*

There are more things in heaven and earth, Horatio,
Than are dreamt of in your philosophy.

— *Hamlet*

Adversity's Sweet milk, philosophy.

— *Romeo and Juliet*

Hast any philosophy in thee, shepherd?

— *As You Like It*

There is something in this more than
natural, if philosophy could find it out.

— *Hamlet*

Hang up philosophy!
Unless philosophy can make a Juliet.

— *Romeo and Juliet*

Young men, whom Aristotle thought
Unfit to hear moral philosophy.

— *Troilus and Cressida*

PIT

To hell, allegiance! vows, to the blackest devil!
Conscience and grace, to the profoundest pit.

— *Hamlet*

Tut, tut; good enough to toss; food for powder, food for powder; they'll fill a pit as well as better: tush, man, mortal men, mortal men.

— *Henry IV*

PITY

But yet the pity of it, Iago!
O Iago, the pity of it, Iago!

— *Othello*

'Tis true 'tis pity; And pity 'tis 'tis true.

— *Hamlet*

No beast so fierce but knows some touch of pity.

— *Richard III*

The quality of mercy is not strained,
It droppeth as the gentle rain from heaven.

— *Merchant of Venice*

Sweet mercy is nobility's true badge.

— *Titus Andronicus*

I shall despair. There is no creature loves me;
And if I die, no soul will pity me;
Nay, wherefore should they, since that I myself
Find in myself no pity to myself?

— *Richard III*

Is there no pity sitting in the clouds,
That sees into the bottom of my grief?

— *Romeo and Juliet*

My nature is subdu'd
To what it works in, like the dyer's hand;
Pity me, then, and wish I were renew'd.

— *Sonnet-III*

POETRY

O for a muse of fire, that would ascend,
The brightest heaven of invention.

— Henry V

Not marble nor the gilded monuments
of princes, shall outlive this powerful rhyme.

— Sonnet-55

The poet's eye, in a fine frenzy rolling,
Doth glance from heaven to earth, from earth to heaven;
And as imagination bodies forth
The forms of things unknown, the poet's pen
Turns them to shapes, and gives to airy nothing
A local habitation and a name.

— A Midsummer Night's Dream

Mincing Poetry.

— Henry IV

The lunatic, the lover, and the poet
Are of imagination all compact:

— A Midsummer Night's Dream

If I could write the beauty of your eyes
And in fresh numbers number all your grace,
The age to come would say, 'This poet lies;
Such heavenly touches ne'er touch'd earthly faces'

— Sonnet-17

POOR

Poor and content is rich, and rich enough.

— *Othello*

How poor are they that have not patience!
What wound did ever heal but by degrees?

— *Othello*

O world! how apt the poor are to be proud.

— *Twelfth Night*

An honest exceeding poor man.

— *The Merchant of Venice*

If thou art rich, thou'rt poor;
For, like an ass whose back with ingots bows,
Thou bear'st thy heavy riches but a journey,
And death unloads thee.

— *Measure for Measure*

Fairest Cordelia, that art most rich, being poor;
Most choice, forsaken; and most lov'd, despis'd!

— *King Lear*

When that the poor have cried, Caesar hath wept;
Ambition should be made of stener stuff.

— *Julius Caesar*

I am as poor as Job, my lord, but not so patient.

— *Henry IV*

Beggar that I am, I am poor even in thanks.

— *Hamlet*

POSSESSION

An ill-favoured thing, Sir, but mine own.

— As You Like It

Now boast thee, death, in thy possession lies
A lass unparallel'd.

— Antony and Cleopatra

O! cursed, cursed slave, whip me, ye devils,
From the possession of this heavenly sight!
Blow me about in winds! roast me in sulphur!
Wash me in steep-down gulfs of liquid fire!
O Desdemona! Desdemona! dead!

— Othello

Mad in pursuit, and in possession so;
Had, having, and in quest to have, extreme;
A bliss in proof, — and prov'd, a very woe;
Before, a Joy propos'd; behind, a dream.

— Sonnet-129

For it so falls out
That what we have we prize not to the worth
Whiles we enjoy it, but being lack'd and lost,
Why, then we rack the value, then we find
The virtue that possession would not show us,
Whiles it was ours.

— Much Ado About Nothing

POWER

I saw her once
Hop forty paces through the public street;
And having lost her breath, she spoke, and panted
That she did make defect perfection,
And, breathless, power breathe forth.

— *Antony and Cleopatra*

So every bond man in his own hand bears
The power to cancel his captivity.

— *Julius Caesar*

Be bloody, bold and resolute; laugh to scorn
The power of man, for none of woman born
Shall harm Macbeth.

— *Macbeth*

Thou hast not half the power to do me harm
As I have to be hurt.

— *Othello*

They that have power to hurt and will do none,
That do not do the thing they most do show,
Who, moving others, are themselves as stone,
Unmoved, cold, and to temptation slow.

— *Sonnet-94*

PRAYER

My words fly up, my thoughts remain below,
words without thoughts never to heaven go.

— *Hamlet*

His worst fault is that he is given to
prayer. He is something peevish that way.

— *The Merry Wives*

Angels and ministers of grace defend us.

— *Hamlet*

Mount, mount my soul! thy seat is up on high,
Whilst my gross flesh sinks downward, here to die.

— *King Richard II*

Good night, Sweet Prince,
And flights of angels sing thee to thy rest.

— *Hamlet*

He prays but faintly and would be denied.

— *Richard II*

I know thee not, old man; fall to thy prayers;
How it white hairs becomes a fool and Jester!
I have long dream'd of such a kind of man,
So surfeit-swell'd, so old, and so profane.

— *Henry IV*

Now might I do it pat, now he is praying.

— *Hamlet*

PREACHING

If to do were as easy as to know what
were good to do, chapels had been churches
and poor men's cottages princes' palaces.
It is a good divine that follows his own
instructions: I can easier teach twenty
what were good to be done, than be one
of the twenty to follow mine own
teaching.

— *Merchant of Venice*

Do not, as some ungracious pastors do,
Show me the steep and thorny way to heaven;
whiles, like a puff'd and reckless libertine,
Himself the primrose path of dalliance treads
And recks not his own rede.

— *Hamlet*

Sweet are the uses of adversity,
which like the toad, ugly and venomous,
wears yet a precious Jewel in his head:
And this our life, exempt from public haunt,
Finds tongues in trees, books in the running brooks,
Sermons in stones, and good in everything.

— *As You Like It*

PROCRASTINATION

The patient dies while the physician sleeps;
The orphan pines while the oppressor feeds;
Justice is feasting while the widow weeps:
Avarice is sporting while infection breeds.

— *The Rape of Lucrece*

PROFIT

We go to gain a little patch of ground,
That hath in it no profit but the name.

— *Hamlet*

These earthly godfathers of Heaven's lights,
That give a name to every fixed star,
Have no more profit of their shining nights
Than those that walk and wot not what they are.

— *Love's Labour's Lost*

No profit grows where is no pleasure ta'en;
In brief, Sir, study what you most affect.

— *The Taming of the Shrew*

You taught me language; and my profit on't
Is, I know how to curse: the red plague rid you,
For learning me your language!

— *The Tempest*

We, ignorant of ourselves,
Beg often our own harms, which the wise powers
Deny us for our good; so find we profit
By losing of our prayers.

— *Antony and Cleopatra*

PROMISE

And be these juggling fiends no more believ'd,
That patter with us in a double sense.
That keep the word of promise to our ear,
And break it to our hope.

— *Macbeth*

Break an hour's promise in love! He that will divide a minute into a thousand parts, and break but a part of the thousandth part of a minute in the affairs of love, it may be said of him that cupid hath clapped him o'the shoulder, but I'll warrant him heart-whole.

— *As You Like It*

Why didst thou promise such a beauteous day,
And make me travel forth without my cloak?

— *Sonnet-34*

His promises were, as he then was, mighty;
But his performance, as he is now, nothing.

— *Henry VIII*

Thou hast it now: king, cawdor, Glamis, all,
As the weird women promis'd; and, I fear,
Thou play'dst most foully for 't; yet it was said,
It should not stand in thy posterity,
But that myself should be the root and father
of many kings.

— *Macbeth*

PROPHECY

If you can look into the seeds of time,
And say which grain will grow and which will not,
Speak then to me, who neither beg nor fear,
Your favours nor your hate.

— *Macbeth*

O my prophetic soul!
My uncle!

— *Macbeth*

There is a history in all men's lives,
Figuring the nature of the times deceas'd,
The which observ'd, a man may prophesy,
With a near aim, of the main chance of things
As yet not come to life, which in their seeds
And weak beginnings lie intreasured.

— *Henry IV*

The night has been unruly: where we lay
our chimneys were blown down; and, as they say,
Lamentings heard i' the air : strange screame of death,
And prophesying with accents terrible
of dire combustion and confus'd events
Now hatch'd to the woeful time.

— *Macbeth*

PROVIDENCE

There's a divinity that shapes our ends,
Rough-hew them how we will.

— Hamlet

He that doth the ravens feed
Yea, providentially caters for the sparrow,
Be comfort to my age!

— As You Like It

Not a whit, we defy augury; there's a special providence in the fall of a sparrow. If it be now, 'tis not to come; if it be not to come, it will be now; if it be not now, yet it will come; the readiness is all.

— Hamlet

PURE

Be thou as chaste as ice, as pure as snow,
thou shalt not escape calumny.

— *Hamlet*

O! throw away the worser part of it,
A live the purer with the other half.

— *Hamlet*

QUARREL

Beware
of entrance to a quarrel; but being in,
Bear't that the opposed may beware of thee.

— *Hamlet*

.......we quarrel in print, by the book;........
The first, the Retort Courteous; the second,
the quip modest; the third, the Reply churlish;
the fourth, the reproof valiant; the fifth, the
Countercheck quarrel some; the sixth, the Lie
with circumstance; the seventh, the Lie
Direct. All these you may avoid but the Lie
Direct; and you may avoid that too, with
an if...........

— *As You Like It.*

Rightly to be great
Is not to stir without great argument,
But greatly to find quarrel in a straw
when honour's at the stake.

— *Hamlet*

In a false quarrel there is no true valour.

— *Much Ado About Nothing*

For several virtues
Have I lik'd several women; never any
with so full soul but some defect in her
Did quarrel with the noblest grace she ow'd,
And put it to the foil.

— *The Tempest*

RAIN

When that I was and a little tiny boy,
with hey, ho, the wind and the rain,
A foolish thing was but a toy,
For the rain it raineth every day.

— *Twelfth Night*

That Sir which serves and seeks for gain,
And follows but for form,
Will pack when it begins to rain,
And leave thee in the storm.

— *King Lear*

Most excellent accomplished lady, the
heavens rain odours on you!

— *Twelfth Night*

What should we speak of
When we are old as you? when we shall hear,
The hair and wind beat dark December, how,
In this our pinching cave, shall we discourse,
The freezing hours away?

— *Cymbeline*

The quality of mercy is not strain'd,
It droppeth as the gentle rain from heaven
Upon the place beneath: it is twice bless'd;
It blesseth him that gives and him that takes.

— *The Merchant of Venice*

RELIEF

For this relief much thanks: 'tis bitter cold,
And I am sick at heart.

— *Hamlet*

Now, good Cesario, but that piece of song,
That old and antique song we heard last night;
Methought it did relieve my passion much,
More than light airs and recollected terms,
Of these most brisk and giddy-paced times;
Come, but one verse.

— *Twelfth Night*

The spinsters and the knitters in the sun
And the free maids that weave their thread with bones,
Do use to chant it: it is silly sooth,
And dallies with the innocence of love,
Like the old age.

— *Twelfth Night*

As a decrepit father takes delight
To see his active child do deeds of youth,
So I, made lame by fortune's dearest spite,
Take all my comfort of thy worth and truth.

— *Sonnet-37*

Of comfort no man speak;
Let's talk of graves, of worms, and epitaphs:
Make dust our paper, and with rainy eyes
Write sorrow on the bosom of the earth.

— *Richard II*

REMORSE

Stop up the access and passage to remorse,
That no compunctious visitings of nature
shake my fell purpose.

— *Macbeth*

Never pray more; abandon all remorse:
On horror's head horrors accumulate.

— *Othello*

The gaudy, blabbing, and remorseful day
Is crept into the bosom of the sea.

— *Henry VI*

RENOWN

This nurse, this teeming womb of royal kings
Fear'd by their breed and famous by their birth,
Renowned for their deeds as far from home.

— Richard II

Had I but died an hour before this chance,
I had liv'd a blessed time: for, from this instant,
There's nothing serious in mortality:
All is but toys: renown and grace is dead,
The wine of life is drawn, and the mereless
Is left this vault to brag of.

— Macbeth

REPUTATION

Seeking the bubble reputation
Even in the cannon's mouth.

— As You Like It

Who steals my purse steals trash; . . .
But he that filches from me my good name
Robs me of that which not enriches him,
And makes me poor indeed.

— Othello

Reputation, reputation, reputation! O! I have lost my reputation. I have lost the immortal part of myself, and what remains is bestial. My reputation, Iago, my reputation!

— Othello

The purest treasure mortal times afford
Is spotless reputation; that away,
Men are but gilded loam or painted clay.
A Jewel in a ten-times-barr'd-up chest
Is a bold spirit in a loyal breast.
Mine honour is my life; both grow in one:
Take honour from me, and my life is done.

— King Richard II

RESOLUTION

And thus the native hue of resolution
Is sicklied o'er with the pale cast of thought.

— *Hamlet*

Shall there be gallows standing in England
When thou art king, and resolution thus
fobbed as it is with the rusty curb of
old father antick, the law?

— *Henry IV*

I pull in resolution, and begin
To doubt the equivocation of the fiend
That lies like truth: 'Fear not, till Birnam wood,
Do come to Dunsinane;

— *Macbeth*

But let determin'd things to destiny
Hold unbewail'd their way.

— *Antony and Cleopatra*

Farewell! thou art too dear for my possessing,
And like enough thou know'st thy estimate:
The charter of thy worth gives thee releasing:
My bonds in thee are all determinate.

— *Sonnet-87*

REST

Quietness, grown sick of rest, would purge
By any desperate change.

— Antony and Cleopatra

Rest, rest, perturbed spirit!

— Hamlet

We should profane the service of the dead,
To sing a requiem, and such rest to her,
As to peace-parted souls.

— Hamlet

The rest is silence.

— Hamlet

So may he rest; his faults lie gently on him!

— Henry VIII

Sleep dwell upon thine eyes, peace in thy breast!
Would I were sleep and peace, so sweet to rest!

— Romeo and Juliet

Now cracks a noble heart. Good-night, sweet prince,
And flights of angels sing thee to thy rest!

— Hamlet

RETRIBUTION

For 'tis sport to have the engineer
Hoist with his own petar.

— *Hamlet*

Things past redress are now with me past care.

— *Richard II*

RETURN

O! call back yesterday, bid time return.

— *Richard II*

I am in blood
Stepp'd in so far that, should I wade no more,
Returning were as tedious as go o'er.

— *Macbeth*

REVENGE

If I can catch him once upon the hip,
I will feed fat the ancient grudge I bear him.

— *Merchant of Venice*

If a Jew wrong a Christian, what is his humility? Revenge. If a Christian wrong a Jew, what should his suffrance be by Christian example? why, revenge. The villainy you teach me, I will execute, and it shall go hard but I will better the instruction.

— *Merchant of Venice*

Not Cassio kill'd! then murder's out of tune,
And sweet revenge grows harsh.

— *Othello*

Had all his hairs been lives, my great revenge
Had stomach for them all.

— *Othello*

Revenge his foul and most unnatural murder.

— *Hamlet*

By this leek, I will most horribly revenge.

— *Henry V*

Caesar's spirit, ranging for revenge,
with Ate by his side, come hot from hell,
shall in these confines, with a monarch's voice
cry, "Havoc!" and let slip the dogs of war.

— *Julius Caesar*

RUMOUR

Rumour is a pipe
Blown by surmises, Jealousies, conjectures

— Henry IV

Whose edge is sharper than the sword, whose tongue
outvenoms all the worms of Nile, whose breath,
Rides on the posting winds and doth belie
All corners of the world: kings, queens and States,
Maids, matrons, nay, the secrets of the grave
This viperous slander enters.

— Cymbeline

Make me a willow cabin at your gate,
And call upon my soul within the house;
Write loyal cantons of contemned love,
And sing them loud even in the dead of night;
Hallow your name to the reverberate hills,
And make the babbling gossip of the air
Cry out, 'olivia'.

— Twelfth Night

RUN

Run, run, orlando: carve on every tree
The fair, the chaste, and unexpressive she.

— As You Like It

But I will be
A bridegroom in my death, and run into 't
As to a lover's bed.

— Antony and Cleopatra

SAFETY

........Out of this nettle, danger, we pluck
this flower, safety.

— Henry IV

His greatness weigh'd, his will is not his own,
For he himself is subject to his birth;
He may not, as unvalu'd persons do,
Carve for himself, for on his choice depends
The safety and the health of the whole State.

— Hamlet

I speak of peace, while covert enmity
Under the smile of safety wounds the world.

— Henry IV

I would give all my fame for a pot c- ale, and safety.

— Henry V

In her days every man shall eat in safety
Under his own vine what he plants; and sing
The merry songs of peace to all his neighbours.

— Henry VIII

The wound of peace is surety,
Surety secure.

— Troilus and Cressida

SEA

Since brass, nor stone, nor earth, nor boundless sea,
But sad mortality o'ersways their power,
How with this rage shall beauty hold a plea,
Whose action is no stronger than a flower?

— *Sonnet-65*

Alas! their love may be call'd appetite,
No motion of the liver, but the palate,
That suffer surfeit, cloyment, and revolt;
But mine is all as hungry as the sea,
And can digest so much.

— *Twelfth Night*

Bohemia. A desert country near the sea.

— *The Winter's Tale*

The sea being smooth
How many shallow bauble boats dare sail
Upon her patient breast.

— *Troilus and Cressida*

Now would I give a thousand furlongs
Of sea for an acre of barren ground.

— *The Tempest*

The time and my intents are savage-wild,
More fierce and more inexorable far
than empty tigers or the roaring sea.

— *Romio and Juliet*

England, bound in with the triumphant sea.

— *Richard II*

I would not my unhoused free condition
Put into circumscription and confine
For the sea's worth.

— *Othello*

Ornament is but the guilded shore
To a most dangerous sea.

— *The Merchant of Venice*

The sea, with such a storm as his bare head
In hell — black night endur'd, would have buoy'd up,
And quench'd the stelled fires.

— *King Lear*

The gaudy, blabbing and remorseful day
Is crept into the bosom of the sea.

— *Henry VI*

And make your chronicle as rich with praise
As is the owse and bottom of the sea
with sunken wrack and sumless treasuries.

— *Henry V*

Whether in sea or fire, in earth or air,
The extravagant and erring spirit hies,
To his confine.

— *Hamlet*

SELF

Our remedies oft in ourselves do lie

— All's Well That Ends Well

This above all: To thine own self be true,
And it must follow, as the night the day,
Thou canst not then be false to any man.

— Hamlet

I bear a charmed life.

— Macbeth

Allowing him a breath, a little scene,
To monarchize, be fear'd, and kill with looks,
Infusing him with self and vain conceit
As if this flesh which walls about our life
Were brass impregnable; and humour'd thus
comes at the last, and with a little pin
Bores through his castle wall, and farewell king!

— Richard II

Do not swear at all;
Or, if thou wilt, swear by thy gracious self,
which is the god of my idolatry.

— Romeo and Juliet

O! you are sick of self-love, Malvolio.

— Twelfth Night

SERVICE

Had I but served my God with half the zeal
I served my king, he would not in mine age
Have left me naked to mine enemies.

— *Henry VIII*

O good old men, how well in thee appears
The constant service of the antique world,
When service sweat for duty, not for meed!

— *As You Like It*

Though in the trade of war I have slain men,
Yet do I hold it very stuff o' the conscience
To do no contriv'd murder: I lack iniquity
Sometimes to do me service.

— *Othello*

You know that love
will creep in service where it cannot go.

— *The Two Gentlemen of Verona*

Beauty, wit,
High birth, vigour of bone, desert in service,
Love, friendship, charity, are subjects all
To envious and calumniating time.
One touch of nature makes the whole world kin,
That all with one consent praise new-born gawds.

— *Troilus and Cressida*

SHADOW

Some there be that shadows kiss;
Such have but a shadow's bliss.

— Merchant of Venice

In such a night
Did this be fearfully o'ertrip the dew,
And saw the lion's shadow ere himself,
And ran dismay'd away.

— The Merchant of Venice

Out, out, brief candle!
Life's but a walking shadow, a poor player,
That struts and frets his hour upon the stage,
And then is heard no more; it is a tale
Told by an idiot, full of sound and fury,
Signifying nothing.

— Macbeth

The very substance of the ambitious
is merely the shadow of a dream.

— Hamlet

A dream itself is but a shadow.

— Hamlet

Show his eyes, and grieve his heart;
Come like shadows, so depart!

— Macbeth

SHAME

He was not born to shame:
Upon his brow shame is ashamed to sit.

— Romeo and Juliet

Too much of water hast thou, poor ophelia,
And therefore I forbid my tears; but yet
It is our trick, nature her custom holds,
Let shame say what it will.

— Hamlet

O! while you live, tell truth, and shame the devil!

— Henry IV

But I'll not chide thee;
Let shame come when it will, I do not call it:
I do not bid the thunder-bearer shoot,
Nor tell tales of thee to high-Judging Jove.

— King Lear

I do not think a braver gentleman
More active-valiant or more valiant-young,
More daring or more bold, is now alive
To grace this letter age with noble deeds,
For my part, I may speak it to my shame,
I have a truant been to chivalry.

— Henry IV

SHEEP

My flocks feed not,
My ewes breed not,
My rams speed not,
All is amiss.

— *The Passionate Pilgrim*

I am a tainted wether of the flock,
Meetest for death.

— *Merchant of Venice*

Gives not the hawthorn bush a sweeter shade
To shepherds, looking on their silly sheep,
Than doth a rich embroider'd canopy
To kings that fear their subjects' treachery?

— *Henry VI*

Is it not strange that sheep's guts
Should hale souls out of men's bodies?

— *Much Ado About Nothing*

SHINE

He made me mad
To see him shine so brisk, and smell so sweet.

— Henry IV

The skies are painted with unnumber'd sparks,
They are all fire and every one doth shine,
But there's but one in all doth hold his place:

— Julius Caesar

SHIPWRECK

Methought I saw a thousand fearful wrecks:
Ten thousand men that fishes gnaw'd upon;
Wedges of gold, great anchors, heaps of pearl,
Inestimable stones, unvalued Jewels,
All scattered in the bottom of the sea.

— *Richard III*

SHORE

Sigh no more, ladies, sigh no more,
men were deceivers ever;
One foot in sea, and one on shore,
To one thing constant never.

— *Much Ado About Nothing*

Like as the waves make towards the pebbled shore,
So do our minutes hasten to their end.

— *Sonnet-60*

The throne he sits on, nor the tide of pomp
That beats upon the high shore of this world.

— *Henry V*

Ornament is but the guiled shore
To a most dangerous sea.

— *The Merchant of Venice*

SIN

I am a man
more sinned against than sinning.

— *King Lear*

Some rise by sin, and some by virtue fall.

— *Measure for Measure*

The oldest sins the newest kind of ways

— *King Henry IV*

Commit
The oldest sins the newest kind of ways.

— *Henry IV*

It's a bawdy planet.

— *The Winter's Tale*

O, fie, fie, fie!
Thy sin's not accidental, but a trade.

— *Measure for Measure*

Nothing emboldens sin so much as mercy.

— *Timon of Athens*

Virtue that transgresses is but patched with sin; and sin that amends is but patched with virtue.

— *Twelfth Night*

Well, whiles I am a beggar, I will rail,
And say there is no sin, but to be rich;
And, being rich, my virtue then shall be,
To say there is no vice, but beggary.

— *King John*

SING

Come, let's away to prison;
We two alone will sing like birds i' the cage;

— *King Lear*

Sing no more ditties, sing no more
Of dumps so dull and heavy:

— *Much Ado About Nothing*

O, she will sing the savageness out of a bear.

— *Othello*

The white sheet bleaching on the hedge,
With heigh! the sweet birds, o, how they sing!
Doth set my pugging tooth on edge;
For a quart of ale is a dish for a king.

— *The Winter's Tale*

O! stay and hear; your true love's coming,
That can sing both high and low.

— *Twelfth Night*

Write loyal cantons of contemned love,
And sing them loud even in the dead of night;

— *Twelfth Night*

Orpheus with his lute made trees,
And the mountain-tops that freeze,
Bow themselves when he did sing:

— *Henry VIII*

SLANDER

Whose edge is sharper than the sword, whose tongue
Outvenoms all the worms of Nile, whole breath
Rides on the posting winds and doth belie
All corners of the world; kings, queens and States,
Maids, matrons, nay, the secrets of the grave,
This viperous slander enters.

— *Cymbeline*

I would not, in plain terms, from this time forth,
Have you so slander any moment's leisure.

— *Hamlet*

Fear no more the lightning flash,
Nor the all-dreaded thunder-stone;
Fear not slander, censure rash;
Thou hast finish'd Joy and moan;
All lovers young, all lovers must
Consign to thee, and come to dust.

— *Cymbeline*

I will be hang'd, if some eternal villain,
Some busy and insinuating rogue,
Some cogging cozening slave, to get some office,
Have not devis'd this slander.

— *Othello*

SLEEP

O sleep, thou ape of death, lie dull upon her!
And be her sense but as a monument.

— *Cymbeline*

Canst thou, o partial sleep, give thy repose
To the wet sea-boy in an hour so rude
And in the calmest and most stillest night,
With all appliances and means to boot,
Deny it to a king? Then happy low, lie down!
Uneasy lies the head that wears a crown.

— *Henry IV*

O sleep, O gentle sleep,
Nature's soft nurse, how hate I frighted thee,
That now no more wilt weight my eyelids down
And steep my senses in forgetfulness?

— *Henry IV*

Not poppy nor mandragora,
Nor all the drowsy syrups of the world,
Shall ever medicine thee to that sweet sleep
which thou ow'dst yesterday.

— *Othello*

Methought I heard a voice cry, "sleep no more!
Macbeth doth murder sleep," the innocent sleep,
Sleep that knits up the ravell'd sleave of care,
The death of each day's life, sore labour's bath,
Balm of hurt minds, great nature's second course,
chief nourisher of life's feast.

— *Macbeth*

Glamis hath murder'd sleep, and therefore cawdor
Shall sleep no more, Macbeth shall sleep no more!

— *Macbeth*

But, I pray you, let none of your people
Stir me; I have an exposition of sleep come upon me.

— *A Midsummer Night's Dream*

Some come to take their ease
And sleep an act or two.

— *Henry VIII*

Thy ignominy sleep with thee in the grave,
But not remember'd in thy epitaph!
What! old acquaintance! could not all this flesh,
Keep in a little fire? poor Jack, farewell!
I could have better spar'd a better man.

— *Henry IV*

You lack the season of all natures, sleep.

— *Macbeth*

Sleep shall neither night nor day
Hang upon his pent-house lid.

— *Macbeth*

Shake off this downy sleep, death's counterfeit,
And look on death itself! up, up, and see
The great doom's image!

— *Macbeth*

Thou hast nor your nor age;
But, as it were, an after-dinner's sleep,
Dreaming on both.

— *Measure for Measure*

Peace shall go sleep with Turks and infidels.

— *Richard II*

Sleep dwell upon thine eyes, peace in thy breast!
Would I were sleep and peace, so sweet to rest!

— *Romeo and Juliet*

For the life to come, I sleep out the thought of it.

— *The Winter's Tale*

Sleep rock thy brain;
And never come mischance between us twain!

— *Hamlet*

O polish'd perturbation! golden care!
That keep'st the ports of slumber open wide
To many a watchful night! sleep with it now!

— *Henry IV*

SMILE

One may smile, and smile, and be a villain.

— Hamlet

I speak of peace, while covert enmity
Under the smile of safety wounds the world.

— Henry IV

Seldom he smiles, and smiles in such a sort
As if he mock'd himself, and scorn'd his spirit,
That could be mov'd to smile at anything.

— Julius Caesar

Nature hath fram'd strange fellows in her time;
So that will evermore peep through their eyes
And laugh like parrots at a bagpiper;
And other of such vinegar aspect
That they'll not show their teech in way of smile,
Though Nestor swear the Jest be laughable.

— The Merchant of Venice

Think not, thou noble Roman,
That ever Brutus will go bound to Rome;
He bears too great a mind; but this same day must end that work the idea of march begun;
And whether we shall meet again, I know not.
Therefore our everlasting farewell take;
For ever, and for ever, farewell, Cassius!
If we do meet again, why, we shall smile
If not, why then, this parting was well made.

— Julius Caesar

SOLDIER

A soldier,
Full of strange oaths and bearded like the pard,
Jealous in honour, sudden and quick in quarrel,
Seeking the bubble reputation
Even in the cannon's mouth.

— *As You Like It*

He's a tried and valiant soldier.

— *Julius Caesar*

That in the captain's but a choleric word,
Which in the soldier is flat blasphemy.

— *Measure for Measure*

And let me the canakin clink;
A soldier's a man;
A life's but a span;
Why then let a soldier drink.

— *Othello*

But we are soldiers;
And may that soldier a mere recreant prove,
That means not, hath not, or is not in love!

— *Troilus and Cressida*

Ambition,
The soldier's virtue.

— *Antony and Cleopatra*

O! wither'd is the garland of the war,
The soldier's pole is fall'n; young boys and girls
Are level now with men; the odds is gone,
And there is nothing left remarkable
Beneath the visiting moon.

— *Antony and Cleopatra.*

SON

O loard, my boy, my Arthur, my fair son!
My life, my joy, my food, my all the world!
My window-comfort, and my sorrow's cure.

— *King John*

In the father the child's image lies.

— *Rape of Lucrece*

When that I was and a little tiny boy,
with hey, ho, the wind and the rain;
A foolish thing was but a toy,
For the rain it raineth every day.

— *Twelfth Night*

I'll be damned for never a king's son in christendom.

— *Henry IV*

This story shall the good man teach his son;
And crispin crispian shall ne'er go by,
From this day to the ending of the world,
But we in it shall be remembered;

— *Henry V*

O mistress mine! where are you roaming?
O! stay and hear: your true love's coming,
That can sing both high and low,
Trip no further, pretty sweeting;
Journeys end in lovers meeting.
Every wise man's son doth know.

— *Twelfth Night*

SORROW

When sorrows come, they come not single spies
But in battalions.

— Hamlet

I cannot choose but weep, to think that they
should lay him i' the cold ground.

— Hamlet

Sweet are the uses of adversity.

— As You Like It

The worst is not
So long as we can say, "This is the worst".

— King Lear

One woe doth tread upon another's heel,
So fast they follow.

— Hamlet

There's small choice in rotten apples.

— The Taming of the Shrew

Misery acquaints a man with strange bed fellows.

— The Tempest

We have seen better days.

— Timon of Athens

A countenance more in sorrow than in anger.

— Hamlet

Down, thou climbing sorrow!
Thy element's below.

— King Lear

SOUL

Ay, springes to catch woodcocks, I do know,
When the blood burns, how prodigal the soul
Lends the tongue vows.

— *Hamlet*

I do not set my life at a pin's fee;
And for my soul, what can it do to that,
Being a thing immortal as itself?

— *Hamlet*

Since my dear soul was mistress of her choice,
And could of men distinguish her election
Hath seal'd thee for herself.

— *Hamlet*

Look, who comes here! a grave unto a soul;
Holding the eternal spirit, against her will,
In the vile prison of afflicted breath,

— *King John*

Thou art a soul in bliss; but I am bound
Upon a wheel of fire, that mine own tears
Do scald like molten lead.

— *King Lear*

I count myself in nothing else so happy
As in a soul remembering my good friends.

— *Richard II*

Make me a willow cabin at your gate,
And call upon my soul within the house;
Write loyal cantons of contemned love,
And sing them loud even in the dead of night;
Halloo your name to the reverberate hills,

And make the babbling gossip of the air
Cry out, 'Olivia'.

— Twelfth Night

I think nobly of the soul, and no way
approve his opinion.

— Twelfth Night

Poor soul, the centre of my sinful earth,
Fool'd by these rebel powers that thee array,
Why dost thou pine within and suffer dearth,
Painting thy outward walls go short a lease,
Dost thou upon thy fading mansion spend?

— Sonnet-146

The soul and body rive not more in parting
Than greatness going off.

— Antony and Cleopatra

O my prophetic soul
My uncle!

— Hamlet

The poor soul sat sighing by a sycamore tree,
Sing all a green willow;
Her hand on her bosom, her head on her knee,
Sing willow, willow, willow!

— Othello

Will you, I pray, demand that demi-devil,
Why he hath thus ensur'd my soul and body?

— Othello

And there at venice gave
His body to that pleasant country's earth,
And his pure soul unto his captain christ,
Under whose colours he had fought so long.

— Richard II

It is my soul that calls upon my name;
How silver-sweet sound lovers' tongues by night,
Like softest music to attending ears!

— *Romeo* and *Juliet*

Women are angels, wooing!
Things won are done; Joy's soul lies in the doing:
That she belov'd knows nought that knows not this;
Men prize the thing ungain'd more than it is.

— *Troilus and Cressida*

Thou almost makest me waver in my faith
To hold opinion with pythagoras
That souls of animals infuse themselves
Into the trunks of men.

— *Merchant of Venice*

Thy soul's flight,
If it find heaven, must find it out to-night.

— *Macbeth*

Is such a night
Troilus methinks mounted the Troyan walls,
And sigh'd his soul toward the Grecian tents,
where Cressid lay that night.

— *The Merchant of Venice*

My parts, my title, and my perfect soul
Shall manifest me rightly.

— *Othello*

The idea of her life shall sweetly creep
Into his study of imagination,
And every lovely organ of her life
Shall come apparell'd in more precious habit,
More moving-delicate, and full of life
Into the eye and prospect of his soul.

— *Much Ado About Nothing*

Excellent wretch! perdition catch my soul
But I do love thee! and when I love thee not,
Chaos is come again.

— *Othello*

SPEECH

Speak the speech, I pray you, as I pronounce
it to you, trippingly on the tongue.

— *Hamlet*

I would be loath to cast away my speech,
For besides that it is excellently well
penned, I have taken great pains to
con it.

— *Twelfth Night*

For I have neither wit, nor words, nor worth,
Action, nor utterance, nor power of speech,
To stir men's blood; I only speak right on;
I tell you that which you yourselves do know.

— *Julius Caesar*

A knavish speech sleep in a foolish ear,

— *Hamlet*

He would drown the stage with tears,
And cleave the general ear with horrid speech,
Make mad the guilty, and appal the free,
Confound the ignorant, and amaze, indeed,
The very faculties of eyes and ears.

— *Hamlet*

Rude am I in my speech,
And little bless'd with the soft phrase of peace;

— *Othello*

SPIRIT

Spirits are not finely touch'd
But to fine issues.

— *Measure for Measure*

I'll break my staff,
Bury it certain fathoms in the earth,
And deeper than did ever plummet sound
I'll drown my book.

— *The Tempest*

GLENDOWER : I can call spirits from the vasty deep.
HOTSPUR : Why so can I, or so can any man;
But will they come when you do call for them?

— *Henry IV*

Double, double toil and trouble,
Fire burn and caldron bubble.

— *Macbeth*

Eye of newt and toe of frog,
Wool of bat and tongue of dog,
Adder's fork and blind worm's sting,
Lizard's leg and owlet's wing,
For a charm of powerful trouble,
Like a hell broth boil and bubble.

— *Macbeth*

Angels and ministers of grace defend us!
Be thou a spirit of health or goblin damn'd,
Bring with thee airs from heaven or blasts from hell,
By thy intents wicked or charitable,
Thou com'st in such a questionable shape

That I will speak to thee; I'll call thee Hamlet,
King, father; royal Dane, O! answer me:

— *Hamlet*

Ay, but to die, and go we know not where;
To lie in cold obstruction and to rot;
This sensible warm motion to become
A kneaded clod; and the delighted spirit
To bathe in fiery floods, or to reside
In thrilling region of thick-ribbed ice.

— *Measure for Measure*

O thou invisible spirit of wine! if thou
hast no name to be known by, let us call
thee devil!

— *Othello*

O spirit of love! how quick and fresh art thou,
That notwithstanding thy capacity
Receiveth as the sea, nought enters there,
Of what validity and pitch soe'er,
But falls into abatement and low price,
Even in a minute: so full of shapes is fancy,
That it alone is high fantastical.

— *Twelfth Night*

From you have I been absent in the spirit,
When proud-pied April, dress'd in all his trim,
Hath put a spirit of youth in every thing.

— *Sonnet-98*

Till that Bellona's bridegroom, lapp'd in proof,
Confronted him with self-comparisons,
Point against point, rebellious arm 'gainst arm,
Curbing his lavish spirit.

— *Macbeth*

Had she been ligh, like you,
Of such a merry, nimble, stirring spirit,
She might ha' been a grandam ere she died;
And so may you; for a light heart lives long.

— *Love's Labour's Lost*

Rest, rest, perturbed spirit!

— Hamlet

A rarer spirit never
Did steer humanity : but you, gods, will give us
Some faults to make us men.

— Antony and Cleopatra

Whether in sea or fire, in earth or air,
The extravagant and erring spirit hies
To his confine.

— Hamlet

I see you stand like grey hounds in the slips,
Straining upon the start. The game's afoot;
Follow your spirit; and, upon this charge
Cry 'God for Harry! England and Saint George!"

— Henry V

SPRING

When daffodils begin to peer
With heigh! the doxy over the dale,
Why, then comes in the sweet o' the year;
For the red blood reigns in the winter's pale.

— *Winter's Tale*

Who are the violets now
That strew the green lap of the new come spring?

— *Richard II*

See, where she comes apparell'd like the spring.

— *Pericles*

O! how this spring of love resembleth
The uncertain glory of an April day.

— *Two Gentlemen of Verona*

It was a lover and his lass,
With a hey, and a ho, and a hey nonino,
That o'er the green cornfield did pass,
In the spring time, the only pretty ring time,
When birds do sing, hey ding a ding, ding;
Sweet lovers love the spring.

— *As You Like It*

Orpheus with his lute made trees,
And the mountain-tops that freeze,
Bow themselves when he did sing;
To his music plants and flowers
Ever sprung: as sun and showers
There had made a lasting spring.

— *Henry VIII*

STARS

There's husbandry in heaven:
Their candles are all out.

— Macbeth

Lord Hamlet is a prince, out of thy star.

— Hamlet

The moist star
Upon whose influence Neptune's empire stands
was sick almost to doomsday with eclipse.

— Hamlet

An admirable evasion of whoremaster
man, to lay his goatish disposition to
the charge of a star!

— King Lear

Look, the unfolding star calls up the shepherd.

— Measure for Measure

There was a star danced, and under that was I born.

— Much Ado About Nothing

She speaks poniards, and every word
stabs: if her breath were as terrible as
her terminations, there were no living
near her; she would infect to the north star.

— Much Ado About Nothing

These earthly godfathers of Heaven's lights
That give a name to every fixed star,
Have no more profit of their shining nights
Than those that walk and wot not what they are.

— Love's Labour's Lost

STORM

Blow, winds, and crack your cheeks! rage! blow!
You cataracts and hurricanes, spout
Till you have drenched our steeples.

— King Lear

An old man, broken with the storms of State
Is come to lay his weary bones among ye;
Give him a little earth for charity.

— Henry VIII

The sea, with such a storm as his bare head,
In hell-black night endur'd, would have bouy'd up,
And quench'd the stelled fires.

— King Lear

Methinks I am a prophet new inspir'd,
And thus expiring do foretell of him;
His rash fierce blaze of riot cannot last,
For violent fires soon burn out themselves;
Small showers last long, but sudden storms are short;
He tries betimes that spurs too fast betimes.

— Richard II

We cannot call her winds and waters
Sighs and tears; they are greater
Storms and tempests than almanacs
can report.

— Antony and Cleopatra.

STRENGTH

O, it is excellent
To have a giant's strength: but it is tyrannous,
To use it like a giant.

— *Measure for Measure*

You do unbend your noble strength to think
So brainsickly of things.

— *Macbeth*

The king's name is a tower of strength.

— *Richard III*

Or as one nail by strength drives out another,
So the remembrance of my former love,
Is by a newer object quite forgotten.

— *Two Gentlemen of Verona*

Well, I'll repent, and that suddenly, while
I am in some liking; I shall be out
Of heart shortly, and then I shall have
no strength to repent.

— *Henry IV*

Nor stony tower, nor walls of beaten brass,
Nor airless dungeon, nor strong links of iron,
Can be retentive to the strength of spirit;

— *Julius Caesar*

SUICIDE

To be or not to be : that is the question:
Whether 'tis nobler in the mind to suffer
The slings and arrows of outrageous fortune,
Or to take arms against a sea of troubles,
And by opposing end them.

— *Hamlet*

It is silliness to live when to live is torment.

— *Othello*

SUMMER

Now is the winter of our discontent
Made glorious summer by this sun of york.

— Richard III

Three winters cold
Have from the forests shook three summers' pride,
Three beauteous springs to yellow autumn turn'd
In process of the seasons have I seen,
Three April perfumes in three hot Junes burn'd,
Since first I saw you fresh, which yet are green,

— Sonnet-104

Farewell, thou latter spring! Farewell,
All — hallown Summer!

— Henry IV

SUN

Hark, hark! the lark at heaven's gate sings,
And Phoebus 'gins arise.

— *Cymbeline*

When the sun shines let foolish gnats make sport,
But creep in crannies when he hides his beams.

— *Comedy of Errors*

The glorious sun
Stays in his course and plays the alchemist,
Turning with splendour of his precious eye
The meagre cloddy earth to glittering gold.

— *King John*

To his music plants and flowers
Ever sprung; as sun and showers
There had made a lasting spring,

— *Henry VIII*

We make guilty of our disasters the
sun, the moon, and the stars; as if we
were villains by necessity, fools by
heavenly compulsion.

— *King Lear*

These late eclipses in the sun and
moon portend to good to us.

— *King Lear*

Mislike me not for my complexion,
The shadow'd livery of the burnished sun.

— *The Merchant of Venice*

See, see, king Rechard doth himself appear,
As doth the blushing discontented sun
From out the fiery portal of the east.

— *Richard II*

Doubt thou the stars are fire;
Doubt that the sun doth move;
Doubt truth to be a liar;
But never doubt I love.

— *Hamlet*

Fear no more the heat o' the sun,
Nor the furious winter's rages;
Thou thy worldly task hast done,
Home art gone and ta'en thy wages;
Golden lads and girls all must,
As chimney-sweepers, come to dust.

— *Cymbeline*

Who doth ambition shun
And loves to live i' the sun,
Seeking the food he eats,
And pleas'd with what he gets.

— *As You Like It*

Hath Britain all the sun that shines?

— *Cymbeline*

Men shut their doors against a setting sun.

— *Timon of Athens*

He jests at scars, that never felt a wound,
But, soft! what light through yonder window breaks?
It is the east, and Juliet is the sun.

— *Romeo and Juliet*

The self-same sun that shines upon his court
Hides not his visage from our cottage, but
Looks on alike.

— *The Winter's Tale*

Against that time when thou shalt strangely pass,
And scarcely greet me with that sun, thine eye,

When love, converted from the thing it was,
Shall reasons find of settled gravity.

— *Sonnet-49*

My mistress' eyes are nothing like the sun;
Coral is far more red than her lips' red;
If snow be white, why then her breast are dun;
If hairs be wires, black wires grow on her head.

— *Sonnet-130*

I 'gin to be aweary of the sun,
And wish the estate o' the world were now undone.

— *Macbeth*

'Tis true; there's magic in the web of it;
A sibyl, that had number'd in the world
The sun to course two hundred compasses,
In her prophetic fury sew'd the work;
The worms were hallow'd that did breed the silk,
And it was dy'd in mummy which the skilful
Conserv'd of maidens' hearts.

— *Othello*

Now is the winter of our discontent
Made glorious summer by this sun of York.

— *Richard III*

Give me my Romeo; and, when he shall die,
Take him and cut him out in little stars,
And he will make the face of heaven so fine
That all the world will be in love with night,
And pay no worship to the garish sun.

— *Romeo and Juliet*

Why, so this gallant will command the sun.

— *The Taming of the Shrew*

SWAN

All the water in the ocean
Can never turn the swan's black legs to white,
Although she lave them hourly in the flood.

— Titus Andronicus

I will play the swan,
And die in music,

— Othello

So doth the swan her downy cygnets save,
Keeping them prisoners underneath her wings,

— Henry VI

The swan's down-feather,
That stands upon the swell at full of tide,
And neither way inclines.

— Antony and Cleopatra

He makes a swan-like end
Fading in music.

— The Merchant of Venice

SWEET

What's in a name? that which we call a rose
By any other name would smell as sweet.

— *Romeo and Juliet*

O thou weed!
Who art so lovely fair and smell'st so sweet
That the sense aches at thee, would thou
hadst ne'er been born!

— *Othello*

TEARS

If you have tears, prepare to shed them now.

— Julius Caesar

Her salt tears fell from her, and soften'd the stones;
Sing willow, willow, willow;
Sing all a green willow must be my garland.

— Othello

With mine own tears I wash away my balm,
With mine own hands I give away my crown.

— Richard II

What potions have I drunk of siren tears,
Distill'd from limbecks foul as hell within.

— Sonnet-119

And all my mother came into mine eyes
And gave me up to tears.

— Henry V

Too much of water hast thou, poor ophelia,
And therefore I forbid my tears; but yet,
It is our trick, nature her custom holds,
Let shame say what it will.

— Hamlet

He would drown the stage with tears,
And cleave the general ear with horrid speech,
Make mad the guilty, and appal the free,
Confound the ignorant, and amaze, indeed,
The very faculties of eyes and ears.

— Hamlet

THOUGHT

Yond cassius has a lean and hungry look;
He thinks too much: such men are dangerous.

— *Julius Caesar*

There is nothing either good or bad but
thinking makes it so.

— *Hamlet*

Give thy thoughts no tongue
Nor any unproportion'd thought his act.

— *Hamlet*

Thy wish was father, Harry, to that thought.

— *Henry IV*

Never a man's thought in the world keeps
the road-way better than thine.

— *Henry IV*

That's a fair thought to lie between maids' legs.

— *Hamlet*

These deeds must not be thought
After these ways; so, it will make us mad.

— *Macbeth*

For the life to come, I sleep out the thought of it.

— *The Winter's Tale*

Young men, whom Aristotle thought
Unfit to hear moral philosophy.

— *Troilus and Cressida*

Flout 'em, and Scout 'em; and scout 'em,
and flout 'em;
Thought is free.

— *The Tempest*

TIDE

There is a tide in the affairs of men,
Which, taken at the flood, leads on to fortune.

— Julius Caesar

O! pardon me, thou bleeding piece of earth,
That I am meeck and gentle with these butchers;
Thou art the ruins of the noblest man
That ever lived in the tide of times.

— Julius Caesar

This common body,
Like to a vagabond flag upon the stream,
Goes to and back, lackeying the varying tide,
To rot itself with motion.

— Antony and Cleopatra

The swan's down-feather,
That stands upon the swell at full of tide,
And neither way inclines.

— Antony and Cleopatra

He's in Arthur's bosom, if ever man
went to Arthur's bosom. A' made a
finer end, and went away and it had
been any christom child; a' parted
even just between twelve and one, even
at the turning o' the tide: for after
I saw him fumble with the sheets
and play with flowers and smile upon
his fingers' ends, I knew there was
but one way; for his nose was as
sharp as a pen, and a' babbled of green fields.

— Henry V

TIME

In the dark backward and abysm of time.

— *The Tempest*

Thus the whirligig of time begins in his revenges.

— *Twelfth Night*

The inaudible and noiseless foot of time.

— *All's Well That Ends Well*

I wasted time, and now doth time waste me.

— *Richard II*

Come what come may,
Time and the hour runs through the roughest day.

— *Macbeth*

This day I breathed first; time is come round,
And where I did begin, there shall I end;
My life is run his compass.

— *Julius Caesar*

I know not how,
But I do find it cowardly and vile,
For fear of what might fall, so to prevent
The time of life.

— *Julius Caesar*

How long a time lies in one little word!
Four lagging winters and four wanton springs
End in a word; Such is the breath of kings,

— *Richard II*

I see no reason why thou shouldst be
So superfluous to demand the time of the day.

— *Henry IV*

The time is out of joint; o cursed spite,
That ever I was born to set it right!

— Hamlet

Time travels in divers paces with divers persons,
I'll tell you who time ambles withal,
Who Time trots withal, who time
gallops withal, and who he stands still withal.

— As You Like It

To show.....the very age and body of
the time his form and pressure.

— Hamlet

I am very proud, revengeful, ambitious;
with more offences at my beck, than
I have thoughts to put them in,
imagination to give them shape, or
time to act them in, what should such
fellows as I do crawling between
heaven and earth?

— Hamlet

Your face, my thane, is as a book where men
May read strange matters, To beguile the time,
Look like the time; bear welcome in your eye,
Your hand, your tongue: look like the innocent flower,
But be the serpent under't.

— Macbeth

Your Lordship, though not clean past
your youth, hath yet some smack of
age in you, some relish of the saltness
of time.

— Henry IV

Old time the clock-setter, that bald Sexton, Time.

— King John

That we shall die, we know; 'tis but the time
And drawing days out, that men stand upon.

— Julius Caesar

The spirit of time shall teach me speed.

— King John

When I have seen by time's fell hand defac'd
The rich-proud cost of outworn buried age.

— Sonnet-64

Time hath, my lord, a wallet at his back,
Wherein he puts alms for oblivion,
A great-siz'd monster of ingratitudes;
Those scraps are good deeds past; which are devour'd
As fast as they are made, forgot as soon
As done.

— Troilus and Cressida

Live to be the show and gaze o'the time.

— Macbeth

A forted residence 'gainst the tooth of time,
And razure of oblivion.

— Measure for Measure

Away, and mock the time with fairest show;
False face must hide what the false heart doth know.

— Macbeth

If you can look into the seeds of time,
And say which grains will grow and which will not.

— Macbeth

My glass shall not persuade me I am old,
So long as youth and thou are of one date;
But when in thee time's furrows I behold,
Then look I death my days should expiate.

— Sonnet-22

Time's glory is to calm contending kings,
To unmask falsehood, and bring truth to light.

— The Rape of Lucrece

Time doth transfix the flourish set on youth
And delves the parallels in beauty's brow.

— Sonnet-60

Open-ey'd conspiracy
His time doth take.

— The Tempest

Time is like a fashionable host
That slightly shakes his parting guest by the hand,
And with his arms outstretch'd, as he would fly,
Grasps in the comer; welcome ever smiles,
And farewell goes out sighing.

— Troilus and Cressida

The end crowns all,
And that old common arbitrator, time,
will one day end it.

— Troilus and Cressida

How sour sweet music is,
When time is broke, and no proportion kept!
So is it in the music of men's lives.

— Richard II

Old John of Gaunt, time-honour'd Lancaster.

— Richard II

'Tis time; descend; be stone no more; approach.

— The Winter's Tale

Against that time when thou shalt strangely pass,
And scarcely greet me with that sun, thine eyes,
When love, converted from the thing it was,
Shall reasons find of settled gravity.

— Sonnet-49

There are many events in the womb
of time which will be delivered.

— Othello

Is there no respect of place, persons,
nor time, in you?

— Twelfth Night

But thought's the slave of life, and life time's fool;
And time, that takes survey of all the world,
Must have a stop.

— Henry IV

TOMORROW

To-morrow, and to-morrow, and to-morrow,
Creeps in this petty pace from day to day
To the last syllable of recorded time.

— *Macbeth*

Two lads that thought there was no more behind
But such a day to-morrow as to-day,
And to be boy eternal.

— *The Winter's Tale*

Know that to-morrow the last of many battles
We mean to fight.

— *Antony and Cleopatra*

He which hath no stomach to this fight,
Let him depart; his passport shall be made,
And crowns for convoy put into his purse;
We would not die in that man's company
That fears his fellowship to die with us.
This day is called the feast of crispian:
He that outlives this day and comes safe home,
Will stand a tip-toe when this day is nam'd,
And rouse him at the name of crispian.
He that shall live this day, and see old age,
Will yearly on the vigil feast his neighbours,
And say, 'To-morrow is Saint crispian;'

— *Henry V*

TRAVEL

Ay, now I am in Arden : the more fool I;
When I was at home, I was in a better
place : but travellers must be content.

— *As You Like It*

Home-keeping youth have ever homely wits.........
I would rather entreat thy company
To see the wonders of the world abroad
Than, living dully sluggardized at home,
Wear out thy youth with shapeless idleness.

— *Two Gentlemen of Verona*

When I was at home, I was in a better place.

— *As You Like It*

O Sir! you had then left unseen a
wonderful piece of work which not to
have been blessed withal would have
discredited your travel.

— *Antony and Cleopatra*

Why didst thou promise such a beauteous day,
And make me travel forth without my cloak?

— *Sonnet-34*

Now spurs the lated traveller apace
To gain the timely inn.

— *Macbeth*

It is a melancholy of mine own, compounded
of many simples, extracted from many objects,
and indeed the sun dry contemplation of my
travels, which, by often rumination, wraps
me in a most humorous sadness.

— *As You Like It*

TREASON

And from the extremist upward of thy head
To the descent and dust below thy foot,
A most toad-spotted traitor.

— King Lear

There's such divinity doth hedge a king,
That treason can but peep to what it would.

— Hamlet

Suspicion all our lives shall be stuck full of eyes;
For treason is but trusted like the fox,
Who, ne'er so tame, so cherish'd, and lock'd up,
Will have a wild trick of his ancestors.

— Henry IV

O! what a fall was there, my countrymen;
Then I, and you, and all of us fell down,
Whilst bloody treason flourish'd over us.
O! now you weep, and I perceive you feel
The dint of pity; these are gracious drops.

— Julius Caesar

Therefore the poet
Did feign that orpheus drew trees, stones, and floods;
Since nought so stockish, hard, and full of rage,
But music for the time doth change his nature,
The man that hath no music in himself,
Nor is not mov'd with concord of sweet sounds,
Is fit for treasons, stratagems, and spoils;
The motions of his spirit are dull as night,
And his affections dark as Erebus:
Let no such man be trusted.

— The Merchant of Venice

TREE

And turn his merry note
Unto the sweet bird's throat,
Come hither, come hither, come hither;
Here shall he see
No enemy
But winter and rough weather.

— *As You Like It*

Hang there like fruit, my soul,
Till the tree die!

— *Cymbeline*

Rur, run, Orlando : carve on every tree
The fair, the chaste, and unexpressive she.

— *As You Like It*

Therefore the poet
Did feign that orpheus drew tree, stones, and floods;
Since nought so stockish, hard, and full of rage,
But music for the time doth change his nature,.
Nor is not mov'd with concord of sweet sounds,
Is fit for treasons, stratagems, and spoils;
The motions of his spirit are dull as night;
And his affections dark as Erebus;
Let no such man be trusted.

— *The Merchant of Venice*

Sometimes we see a cloud that's dragonish;
A vapour sometime like a bear or lion,
A tower'd citadel, a pendant rock,
A forked mountain, or blue promontory
with trees upon't, that nod unto the world
And mock our eyes with air: thou hast seen these signs;
They are black vesper's pageants.

— *Antony and Cleopatra*

TROUBLE

One woe doth tread upon another's heel,
So fast they follow.

— Hamlet

Sweet are the uses of adversity.

— As You Like It

When sorrow come, they come not single spies,
But in battalions!

— Hamlet

The worst is not
So long as we can say, "This is the worst".

— King Lear

There's small choice in rotten apples.

— The Taming of the Shrew

Misery acquaints a man with strange bed fellows.

— The Tempest

We have seen better days.

— Timon of Athens

A woman mov'd is like a fountain troubled,
Muddy, ill-seeming, thick, bereft of beauty.

— The Taming of the Shrew

Not so sick, my lord,
As she is troubled with thick-coming fancies,
That keep her from her rest.

— Macbeth

TRUST

He's mad that trusts in the tameness of a wolf, a horse's health, a boy's love, or a whore's oath.

— *King Lear*

Ha, ha! what a fool honesty is! and
Trust his sworn brother, a very simple
gentleman!

— *The Winter's Tale*

The expense of spirit in a waste of shame
Is lust in action; and till action, lust
Is perjur'd, murderous, bloody, full of blame,
Savage, extreme, rude, cruel, not to trust.

— *Sonnet-129*

I wonder men dare trust themselves with men.

— *Timon of Athens*

There's no art
To find the mind's construction in the face;
He was a gentleman on whom I built
An absolute trust.

— *Macbeth*

The man that hath no music in himself,
Nor is not mov'd with concord of sweet sounds,
Is fit for treasons, stratagems, and spoils;
The motions of his spirit are dull as night,
And his affections dark as Erebus:
Let no such man be trusted.

— *The Merchant of Venice*

TRUTH

To thine own self be true,
And it must follow, as the night the day,
Thou canst not then be false to any man.

— *Hamlet*

And often times to win us to our harm,
The instruments of darkness tell us truths,
Win us with honest trifles, to betray's
In deeper consequence.

— *Macbeth*

Men should be what they seem.

— *Othello*

Every man has his fault, and honesty is his.

— *Timon of Athens*

Take note, take note, o world!
To be direct and honest is not safe.

— *Othello*

O! while you live, tell truth, and shame the devil!

— *Henry IV*

If circumstances lead me, I will find
where truth is hid, though it were hid indeed
within the centre.

— *Hamlet*

Truth will come to light; murder
cannot be hid long.

— *The Merchant of Venice*

O! how much more doth beauty beauteous seem,
By that sweet ornament which truth doth give!

— *Sonnet-54*

Time's glory is to calm contending kings,
To unmask falsehood, and bring truth to light.

— The Rape of Lucrece

Ornament is but the guiled shore
To a most dangerous sea; the beauteous scarf
Veiling an Indian beauty; in a word,
The seeming truth which cunning times put on
To entrap the wisest.

— The Merchant of Venice

Custom calls me to 't :
What custom wills, in all things should we do't,
The dust on antique time would lie unswept,
And mountainous error be too highly heap'd
For truth to o'er peer.

— Coriolanus

Your bait of falsehood takes this carp of truth.

— Hamlet

When my love swears that she is made of truth,
I do believe her, though I know she lies.

— Sonnet-138

UNIVERSE

This goodly frame, the earth, seems to me
a sterile promontory; this most excellent
canopy, the air, look you, this brave
o'er hanging firmament, this majestical
roof fretted with golden fire, why,
it appears no other thing to me than a
foul and pestilent congregation of vapours.

— *Hamlet*

Now entertain conjecture of a time
when creeping murmer and the poring dark
Fills the wide vessel of the universe.
From camp to camp, through the foul womb of night,
The hum of either army stilly sounds,
That the fix'd sentinels almost receive
The secret whispers of each other's watch,
Fire answers fire, and through their paly flames
Each battle sees the other's umber'd face:
Steed threatens steed, in high and boastful neighs
Piercing the night's dull ear; and from the tents,
The armourers, accomplishing the knights,
with busy hammers closing rivets up,
Give dreadful note of preparation.

— *Henry V*

VARIETY

Age cannot wither her, nor custom stale
Her infinite variety: other women cloy
The appetites they feed; but she makes hungry
Where most she satisfies.

— *Antony and Cleopatra*

VERSE

Tear him for his bad verses, tear
him for his bad verses.

— *Julius Caesar*

He capers, he dances, he has eyes of
youth, he writes verses, he speaks
holidy, he smells April and May.

— *The Merry Wives of Windsor*

Was it the proudful sail of his great verse,
Bound for the prize of all too precious you,
That did my ripe thoughts in my brain inhearse,
Making their tomb the womb wherein they grew?

— *Sonnet-86*

This is the very false gallop of verses.

— *As You Like It*

VICE

The gods are just, and of our pleasant vices
make instruments to plague us.

— King Lear

Virtue itself turns vice, being misapplied;
And vice sometimes by action dignified.

— Romeo and Juliet

If one good deed in all my life I did,
I do repent it from my very soul.

— Titus Andronicus

The evil that men do lives after them,
The good is oft interred with their bones.

— Julius Caesar

The State is the more gracious; for 'tis
a vice to know him.

— Hamlet

For in the fatness of these pursy times,
Virtue itself of vice must pardon beg.

— Hamlet

Well, whiles I am a beggar, I will rail,
And say there is no sin, but to be rich;
And, being rich, my virtue then shall be,
To say there is no vice, but beggary.

— King John

O wretched fool!
That liv'st to make thine honesty a vice.
O monstrous world! Take note, take note, o world!
To be direct and honest is not safe.

— Othello

VILLAIN

O villain, villain, smiling, damned villain!

— *Hamlet*

I am alone the villain of the earth,
And feel I am so most.

— *Antony and Cleopatra*

They brought one pinch, a hungry, lean-fac'd villain,
A mere anatomy, a mounte bank,
A threadbare Juggler, and a fortune teller,
A needy, hollow-ey'd, sharp-looking wretch,
A living-dead man.

— *The Comedy of Errors*

There's ne'er a villain dwelling in all Denmark,
But he's an arrant knave.

— *Hamlet*

I like not fair terms and a villain's mind.

— *The Merchant of Venice*

And therefore, since I cannot prove a lover,
I am determined to prove a villain.

— *Richard III*

Villain and he be many miles asunder.

— *Romeo and Juliet*

My conscience hath a thousand several tongues,
And every tongue brings in a several tale,
And every tale condemns me for a villain.

— *Richard III*

VIRTUE

His virtues
Will plead like angels, trumpet-tongued, against
The deep damnation of his taking-off.

— *Macbeth*

For in the fatness of these pursy times,
Virtue itself of vice must pardon beg.

— *Hamlet*

Well, whiles I am a beggar, I will rail,
And say there is no sin, but to be rich;
And, being rich, my virtue then shall be,
To say there is no vice but beggary.

— *King John*

O! he sits high in all the people's hearts;
And that which would appear offence in us,
His countenance, like richest alchemy,
Will change to virtue and to worthiness.

— *Julius Caesar*

For it so falls out
That what we have we prize not to the worth
Whiles we enjoy it, but being lack'd and lost,
Why, then we rack the value, then we find,
The virtue that possession would not show us,
Whiles it was ours.

— *Much Ado About Nothing*

Virtue! a fag! 'tis in ourselves that we
are thus, or thus.
Our bodies are our gardens, to the
which our wills are gardeners.

— *Othello*

Whose solid virtue
The shot of accident nor dart of chance
Could neither graze nor pierce?

— *Othello*

All places that the eye of heaven visits
Are to a wise man ports and happy havens.
Teach thy necessity to reason thus;
There is no virtue like necessity.

— *Richard II*

Virtue that transgresses is but patched
with sin; and sin that amends is but
patched with virtue.

— *Twelfth Night*

My heart laments that virtue cannot live
Out of the teeth of emulation.

— *Julius Caesar*

VOICE

Her voice was ever soft,
Gentle, and low, an excellent thing in woman.

— *King Lear*

Give every man thy ear, but few thy voice.

— *Hamlet*

I'll speak in a monstrous little voice.

— *A Midsummer Night's Dream*

O! for a falconer's voice,
To lure this tassel-gentle back again.
Bondage is hoarse, and may not speak aloud,
Else would I tear the cave where Echo lies.

— *Romeo* and *Juliet*

I thank you for your voices, thank you,
Your most sweet voices.

— *Coriolanus*

Methought I heard a voice cry, 'sleep no more!'

— *Macbeth*

His legs bestrid the ocean; his rear'd arm
crested the world; his voice was propertied,
As all the tuned spheres, and that to friends:

— *Antony* and *Cleopatra*

WAR

.........Cry "Havoc," and let slip the dogs of war.

— *Julius Caesar*

When the hurly-burly's done,
When the battle's lost and won.

— *Macbeth*

O war, thou son of hell!

— *Henry VI*

Lay on, Macduff,
And damn'd be him that first cries "Hold, enough".

— *Macbeth*

O! wither'd is the garland of the war,
The soldier's pole is fall'n; young boy and girls
Are level now with men; the odds is gone,
And there is nothing left remarkable
Beneath the visiting moon.

— *Antony and Cleopatra*

But when the blast of war blows in our ears,
Then imitate the action of the tiger;

— *Henry V*

This battle fares like to the morning's war,
When dying clouds contend with growing light,
What time the shepherd, blowing of his nails,
Can neither call it perfect day nor night.

— *Henry VI*

WEED

O thou weed,
Who art so lovely fair and smell'st so sweet,
That the sense aches at thee, would thou hadst ne'er been born!

— *Othello*

And duller shouldst thou be than the fat weed,
That rots itself in ease on lethe wharf.

— *Hamlet*

Thus may we gather honey from the weed,
And make a moral of the devil himself.

— *Henry V*

Most subject is the fattest soil to weeds,

— *Henry IV*

Crown'd with rank fumiter and furrow weeds,
With burdocks, hemlock, nettles, cuckoo-flowers,
Darnel, and all the idle weeds that grow
In our sustaining corn.

— *King Lear*

There sleeps Titania some time of the night,
Lull'd in these flowers with dances and delight;
And there the snake throws her enamell'd skin,
Weed wide enough to wrap a fairy in.

— *A Midsummer Night's Dream*

WIFE

You are my true and honourable wife,
As dear to me as are the ruddy drops,
That visit my sad heart.

— Julius Caesar

A fellow almost damn'd in a fair wife.

— Othello

For a light wife doth make a heavy husband.

— The Merchant of Venice

She shall watch all night:
And if she chance to nod I'll rail and brawl,
And with the clamour keep her still awake.
This is the way to kill a wife with kindness.

— The Taming of the Shrew

It seems the marriage with his brother's wife,
Has crept too near his conscience.

— Henry VIII

You swear like a comfit-maker's wife.

— Henry IV

O! he's as tedious
As a tired horse, a railing wife;

— Henry IV

By the world,
I think my wife be honest and think she is not;
I think that thou art Just and think thou art not.

— Othello

WILLOW

The poor soul sat sighing by a Sycamore tree,
Sing all a green willow;
Her hand on her bosom her head on her knee,
Sing willow, willow, willow:
The fresh streams ran by her, and murmur'd her moans;
Sing willow, willow, willow;
Her salt tears fell from her, and soften'd the stones:
Sing willow, willow, willow.

— *Othello*

In such a night
Stood Dido with a willow in her hand,
Upon the wild sea-banks, and waft her love,
To come again to carthage.

— *The Merchant of Venice*

Make me a willow cabin at your gate,
And call upon my soul within the house;
write loyal cantons of contemned love,
And sing them loud even in the dead of night;
Halloo your name to the reverberate hills,
And make the babbling gossip of the air
cry out, 'Olivia'.

— *Twelfth Night*

There is a willow grows aslant a brook,
That shows his hoar leaves in the glassy stream:

— *Hamlet*

WIND

Blow, winds, and crack your cheeks! rage! blow!

— King Lear

I'll blows the wind that profits nobody.

— Henry VI

Through the velvet leaves the wind,
All unseen, 'gan passage find;
That the lover, sick to death,
Wish'd himself the heaven's breath.

— Love's Labour's Lost

Contending with the fretful elements;
Bids the wind blow the earth into the sea,
Or swell the curled waters'bve the main.

— King Lear

There is no terror, Cassius, in your threats;
For I am arm'd so strong in honesty
That they pass by me as the idle wind,
Which I respect not.

— Julius Caesar

Imperious Caesar, dead, and turn'd to clay,
Might stop a hole to keep the wind away.

— Hamlet

I am but mad north-north-west; when
the wind is Southerly, I know a hawk
from a handsaw.

— Hamlet

Blow, blow, thou winter wind,
Thou art not so unkind
As man's ingratitude.

— As You Like It

I must have liberty
Withal, as large a charter as the wind,
To blow on whom I please.

— As You Like It

'Tis in grain, Sir; 'twill endure wind and weather.

— Twelfth Night

My boat sails freely, both with wind and stream.

— Othello

If I do prove her haggard,
Though that her Jesses were my dear heart-strings,
I'd whistle her off and let her down the wind,
To prey at fortune.

— Othello

You are not worth the dust which the rude wind,
Blows in your face.

— King Lear

I saw young Harry, with his beaver on,
His cushes on his thighs, gallantly arm'd,
Rise from the ground like feather'd mercury,
And vaulted with such ease into his seat,
As if an angel dropp'd down from the clouds,
To turn and wind a fiery pegasus,
And witch the world with noble horsemanship.

— Henry IV

WINE

Come, thou monarch of the vine,
Plumpy Bacchus with pink eyne!
In thy fats our cares he drown'd,
With thy grapes our hairs be crown'd:
Cup us, till the world go round!

— Antony and Cleopatra

O thou invisible spirit of wine, if thou hast no name to be known by, let us call the devil.

— Othello

Come, come; good wine is a good familiar creature if it be well used; exclaim no more against it.

— Othello

A man cannot make him laugh; but that's no marvel; he drinks no wine.

— Henry IV

If it be true that 'good wine needs no bush; 'tis true that a good play needs no epilogue.'

— As You Like It

Had I but died an hour before this chance,
I had liv'd a blessed time; for, from this instant,
There's nothing serious in mortality:
All is but toys; renown and grace is dead,
The wine of life is drawn, and the mere lees,
Is left this vault to brag of.

— Macbeth

WINTER

When icicles hang by the wall,
And Dick the shepherd blows his nail,
And Tom bears logs into the hall,
And milk comes frozen home in pail,
When blood is nipp'd and ways be foul,
Then nightly sings the staring owl,
Tu-whit;
Tu-who, a merry note
While greasy Joan doth keel the pot.

— *Love's Labour's Lost*

A sad tale's best for winter.

— *The Winter's Tale*

Here shall he see
No enemy,
But winter and rough weather.

— *As You Like It*

Thou art a summer bird,
Which ever in the haunch of winter sings
The lifting up of day.

— *Henry IV*

Winter's not gone yet, if the wild-geese fly that way.

— *King Lear*

For you there's rosemary and rue; these keep
Seeming and savour all the winter long.

— *The Winter's Tale*

How like a winter hath my absence been
from thee, the pleasure of the fleeting year!
what freezings have I felt, what dark days seen!
what old December's bareness every where!

— *Sonnet-97*

WIT

Better a witty fool than a foolish wit.

— Twelfth Night

How now, wit! whither wander you?

— As You Like It

Brevity is the soul of wit.

— Hamlet

Devise, wit! write, pen! for I am for
whole volumes in folio!

— Love's Labour's Lost

Who wears his wit in his belly, and his
guts in his head.

— Troilus and Cressida

Methinks sometimes I have no more wit
than a Christian or an ordinary man
has; but I am a great eater of beef,
and I believe that does harm to my wit.

— Twelfth Night

This fellow's wise enough to play the fool,
And to do that well craves a kind of wit.

— Twelfth Night

Beauty, wit,
High birth, vigour of bone, desert in service,
Love, friendship, charity, are subjects all
To envious and calumniating time.
One touch of nature makes the whole world kin,
That all with one consent praise new-born gawds.

— Troilus and Cressida

WOMAN

Frailty, thy name is woman.

— *Hamlet*

For women are as roses, whose fair flower
Being once display'd, doth fall that very hour.

— *Twelfth Night*

Who is Silvia? what is she,
That all our Swains commend her?
Holy, fair, and wise is she:
The heaven such grace did lend her,
That she might admired be.

— *Two Gentlemen of Verona*

Her voice was ever soft,
Gentle and low, an excellent thing in woman.

— *King Lear*

She is a woman, therefore may be wooed.
She is a woman, therefore may be won.

— *Titus Andronicus*

She never yet was foolish that was fair.

— *Othello*

Age cannot wither her, nor custom stale
Her infinite variety: other women cloy
The appetites they feed.

— *Antony and Cleopatra*

Kindness in women, not their beauteous looks,
Shall win my love.

— *The Taming of the Shrew*

Let not the heavens hear these tell-tale women,
Rail on the Lord's anointed.

— Richard III

Such duty as the subject owes the prince,
Even such a woman oweth to her husband.

— The Taming of the Shrew

A woman mov'd is like a fountain troubled,
Muddy, ill-seeming, thick, bereft of beauty.

— The Taming of the Shrew

I have no other but a woman's reason;
I think him so, because I think him so.

— Two Gentlemen of Verona

Two loves I have of comfort and despair,
which like two spirits do suggests me still:
The better angel is a man right fair,
The worser spirit a woman colour'd ill.

— Sonnet-144

Is there no way for men to be, but women
Must be half-workers?

— Cymbeline

Do you not know I am a woman?
When I think, I must speak.

— As You Like It

I know that a woman is a dish for the
gods, if the devil dress her not.

— Antony and Cleopatra

I grant I am a woman, but, withal,
A woman that Lord Brutus took to wife:
I grant I am a woman, but, withal,
A woman well-reputed, cato's daughter.
Think you I am no stronger than my sex,
Being so fathered and so husbanded?

— Julius Caesar

Cromwell, I did not think to shed a tear
In all my miseries; but thou hast forc'd me.
Out of thy honest truth, to play the woman.

— *Henry VIII*

O constancy! be strong upon my side:
Set a huge mountain 'tween my heart and tongue;
I have a man's mind, but a woman's might.
How hard it is for women to keep counsel!

— *Julius Caesar*

From women's eyes this doctrine I derive;
They are the ground, the books, the academes,
From whence doth spring the true promethean fire.

— *Love's Labour's Lost*

You should be women,
And yet your beards forbid me to interpret,
That you are so.

— *Macbeth*

A poor lone woman.

— *Henry IV*

A' said once, the devil would have him about women.

— *Henry V*

Not so young, Sir, to love a woman
for singing, nor so old to dote on her
for any thing.

— *King Lear*

For where is any author in the world
Teaches such beauty as a woman's eye?
Learning is but an adjunct to ourself.

— *Love's Labour's Lost*

A pestilent complete knave! and the
woman hath found him already.

— *Othello*

I do attend here on the general,
And think it no addition nor my wish
To have him see me woman'd.

— *Othello*

Was ever woman in this humour woo'd?
Was ever woman in this humour won?

— *Richard III*

Relenting fool, and shallow, changing woman!

— *Richard III*

WOOING

She's beautiful and therefore to be woo'd:
She's a woman, therefore to be won.

— Henry VI

Wooing, wedding, and repending, is as
a scotch jig, a measure, and a
cinque-pace.

— Much Ado About Nothing

Women are angels, wooing:
Things won are done; joy's soul lies in the doing:
That she belov'd knows nought that knows not this:
Men prize the thing ungain'd more than it is.

— Troilus and Cressida

At lovers' perjuries,
They say, Jove laughs. O gentle Romeo!
If thou dost love, pronounce it faithfully:
Or if thou think'st I am too quickly won,
I'll frown and be perverse and say thee nay,
So thou wilt woo; but else, not for the world.
In truth, fair montague, I am too fond.

— Romeo and Juliet

Men are April when they woo, December
when they wed: maids are May when
they are maids, but the sky changes
when they are wives.

— As You Like It

WORD

Words, words, mere words, no matter from the heart.

— *Troilus* and *Cressida*

Thou art not so long by the head as
honorificabilitudinitatibus.

— *Love's Labour's Lost*

Words pay no debts.

— *Troilus* and *Cressida*

What's in a name? That which we call a rose
By any other name would smell as sweet.

— *Romeo* and *Juliet*

Brevity is the soul of wit.

— *Hamlet*

That in the captain's but a choleric word,
Which in the soldier is flat blasphemy.

— *Measure for Measure*

What! man; ne'er pull your hat upon your brows;
Give sorrow words: the grief that does not speak.
Whispers the o'er-fraught heart, and bids it break.

— *Macbeth*

When I would pray and think, I think and pray
To several subjects: Heaven hath my empty words.

— *Measure for Measure*

He words me, girls, he words me, that I should not
Be noble to myself.

— *Antony* and *Cleopatra*

A rhapsody of words.

— *Hamlet*

Suit the action to the word, the word
to the action.

— Hamlet

By my troth, captain, these are very bitter words.

— Henry IV

Men of few words are the best men.

— Henry V

Whate'er you think, good words, I think, were best.

— King John

Sweet words,
Low-crooked curtsies, and base spaniel fawning.

— Julius Caesar

But for your words, they rob the Hybla bees,
And leave them honeyless.

— Julius Caesar

How every fool can play upon the word!

— The Merchant of Venice

Here are a few of the unpleasant'st words
That ever blotted paper!

— The Merchant of Venice

I thank thee, Jew, for teaching me that word.

— The Merchant of Venice

One doth not know
How much an ill word may empoison liking.

— Much Ado About Nothing

And if my word be sterling yet in England.

— Richard II

How long a time lies in one little word!
Four lagging winters and four wanton springs
End in a word; such is the breath of kings.

— Richard II

A word and a blow

— *Romeo and Juliet*

Speaks three or four languages word
for word without book.

— *Twelfth Night*

WORLD

How weary, stale, flat and unprofitable,
Seem to me all the uses of this world.

— Hamlet

All the world's a stage,
And all the men and women merely players:
They have their exits and their entrances:
And one man in his time plays many parts,
His acts being seven ages.

— As You Like It

Why, then the world's mine oyster,
Which I with sword will open.

— Merry Wives of Windsor

This goodly frame, the earth, seems to me a
sterile promontory; this most excellent canopy,
the air, look you, this brave o'er hanging
firmament, this majestical roof fretted with
golden fire, why, it appears no other thing
to me than a foul and pestilent congregation of vapour.

— Hamlet

None, my lord, but that the world's grown honest.

— Hamlet

This world is not for aye, nor 'tis not strange,
That even our love should with our fortunes change.

— Hamlet

The world is not thy friend, nor the world's law.

— Romeo and Juliet

One touch of nature makes the whole world kin,
That all with one consent praise new-born gawds.

— Troilus and Cressida

O brave new world,
That has such people in 't.

— *The Tempest*

All this the world well knows; yet none knows well:
To shun the heaven that leads men to this hell.

— *Sonnet-129*

Nay, had she been true,
If heaven would make me such another world,
Of one entire and perfect chrysolite,
I'd not have sold her for it.

— *Othello*

I hold the world but as the world, Gratiano;
A stage where every man must play a part,
And mine a sad one.

— *The Merchant of Venice*

Vex not his ghost; O! let him pass; he hates him
That would upon the rack of this tough world
stretch him out longer.

— *King Lear*

So runs the world away.

— *Hamlet*

If thus thou vanishest, thou tell'st the world,
It is not worth leave-taking.

— *Antony and Cleopatra*

Read not my blemishes in the world's report;
I have not kept the square, but that to come
Shall all be done by the rune.

— *Antony and Cleopatra*

O infinite virtue! com'st thou smiling from
The world's great snare uncaught?

— *Antony and Cleopatra*

Mad world! mad kings! mad composition!

— *King John*

He gave his honour to the world again,
His blessed part to Heaven, and slept in peace.

— Henry VIII

I speak of peace, while covert enmity,
Under the smile of safety wounds the world.

— Henry IV

Lord, Lord, how this world is given to
lying! I grant you I was down and out
of breath; and so was he: but we rose
both at an instant, and fought a long
hour by shrewbury clock.

— Henry IV

Strives in his little world of man to out scorn,
The to-and-fro conflicting wind and rain.
This night, wherein the cub-drawn bear would couch,
The lion and the belly-pinched wolf keep their fur dry.

— King Lear

When in the world I liv'd, I was the
world's commander;
By east, west, north, and south, I spread
my conquering might;
My scutcheon plain declares that I am Alisander.

— Love's Labour's Lost

How far that little candle throws his beams!
So shines a good deed in a naughty world.

— The Merchant of Venice

Why, then the world's mine oyster,
Which I with sword will open.

— The Merry Wives of Windsor

O, what a world of vile ill-favour'd faults,
Looks handsome in three hundred pounds a year!

— The Merry Wives of Windsor

I have been studying how I may compare
This prison where I live unto the world.

— Richard II

WOUNDS

He jests at scars that never felt a wound.

— Romeo and Juliet

How poor are they that have not patience!
What wound did ever heal but by degrees?

— Othello

I weep for Joy
To stand upon my kingdom once again.
Dear earth, I do salute thee with my hand,
Though rebels wound thee with their horses' hoofs.

— Richard II

The wound of peace is surety,
Surety secure.

— Troilus and Cressida

Poor wounded name! my bosom, as a bed
Shall lodge thee till thy wound be thoroughly heal'd.

— Two Gentlemen of Verona

Horatio, what a wounded name,
Things standing thus unknown, shall live behind me.

— Hamlet

Well, I am loath to gall a new-healed wound.

— Henry IV

But were I Brutus,
And Brutus Antony, there were an Antony
Would ruffle up your spirits, and put a tongue,
In every wound of Caesar, that should move
The stones of Rome torise and mutiny.

— Julius Caesar

YOUTH

Then come kiss me, sweet-and-twenty,
Youth's a stuff will not endure.

— Twelfth Night

My salad days
When I was green in judgment; cold in blood.

— Antony and Cleopatra

Thou hast nor youth nor age;
But, as it were, an after-dinner's sleep,
Dreaming on both.

— Measure for Measure

He capers, he dances, he has eyes of
youth, he writes verses, he speaks
holiday, he smells April and May.

— The Merry Wives of Windsor

Home-keeping youth have ever homely wits.

— Two Gentlemen of Verona

Crabbed age and youth cannot live together;
Youth is full of pleasance, age is full of care.

— The Passionate Pilgrim

Age, I do abhor thee, youth, I do adore thee.

— The Passionate Pilgrim

From you have I been absent in the spring,
When proud-pied April, dress'd in all his trim,
Hath put a spirit of youth in every thing.

— Sonnet-98

SHAKESPEARIAN REFERENCES

Time doth transfix the flourish set on youth
And delves the parallels in beauty's brow.

— Sonnet-60

Your lordship, though not clean past
Your youth, hath yet some smack of
age in you, some relish of the saltness of time.

— Henry IV

He was indeed the glass
Wherein the noble youth did dress themselves.

— Henry IV

A violet in the youth of primary nature,
Forward, not permanent, sweet, not lasting.
The perfume and suppliance of a minute.

— Hamlet

He wears the rose
Of youth upon him.

— Antony and Cleopatra

Though I look old, yet I am strong and lusty:
For in my youth I never did apply
Hot and rebellious liquors in my blood.

— As You Like It

A very riband in the cap of youth.

— Hamlet